Imaginative
WEAVING

Imaginative
WEAVING

Jacqueline Short

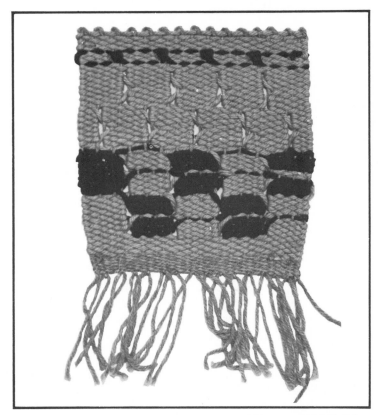

Pitman Publishing

First published 1976

PITMAN PUBLISHING LTD
Pitman House, 39 Parker Street, London WC2B 5PB, UK

PITMAN MEDICAL PUBLISHING CO LTD
42 Camden Road, Tunbridge Wells, Kent TN1 2QD, UK

FOCAL PRESS LTD
31 Fitzroy Square, London W1P 6BH, UK

PITMAN PUBLISHING CORPORATION
6 East 43 Street, New York, NY 10017, USA

FEARON PUBLISHERS INC
6 Davis Drive, Belmont, California 94002, USA

PITMAN PUBLISHING PTY LTD
Pitman House, 158 Bouverie Street, Carlton, Victoria 3053,
Australia

PITMAN PUBLISHING
COPP CLARK PUBLISHING
517 Wellington Street West, Toronto M5V 1G1, Canada

SIR ISAAC PITMAN AND SONS LTD
Banda Street, PO Box 46038, Nairobi, Kenya

PITMAN PUBLISHING CO SA (PTY) LTD
Craighall Mews, Jan Smuts Avenue, Craighall Park, Johannesburg 2001, South Africa

ISBN 0 273 00490 5

Text set in 12/13 pt Photon Imprint, printed by photolithography,
and bound in Great Britain at The Pitman Press, Bath

G6:16

ACKNOWLEDGEMENTS

I would like to thank Nick Claxton and Ian Philip for taking the photographs for this book.
Breda colour studios

Contents

Introduction

Many books on weaving assume a basic knowledge of the craft on the part of the reader. I have tried to avoid this and also the use of too much technical terminology (although some is necessary for clarity), because this can discourage the beginner. You don't need a loom, nor do you need to use a yarn of wool or cotton to produce what is called a piece of weaving. Weaving is a technique of interlacing one set of pliable materials with another set of materials, and this simple definition describes the idea of weaving.

At the beginning of this book looms have been ignored and attention concentrated purely on the interlacing aspects of weaving. It is only later that looms, and then only simple ones, are introduced.

As you begin to develop your own design ideas, don't feel that everything you make should have a use. If you start off with this narrow field of vision, you will never experience any of those lucky flukes that can give rise to a truly creative idea. If an object that you have produced pleases you, let that be reason enough for its existence. Don't get discouraged if you make mistakes. By the time you have tried out some of the ideas in this book, it is hoped that weaving will have become your favourite pastime.

1 Weaving with paper

The warp and the weft

There are two words that you will find frequently mentioned in books on weaving. The *warp* is composed of the long threads that run the length of a fabric and are parallel to the edges or selvedges of the material. The *weft* is composed of the threads that run across the fabric from side to side and interlace with the warp threads.

Plain weaving

The simplest form of weaving is shown in fig. 1. This is plain weaving in which a single thread is passed over and under a series of single threads. The process is repeated on the following row, but where in the previous row the thread passed over a thread it now passes under it, and vice versa.

Plain weaving with paper strips

The easiest type of paper to work with for practice purposes is sticky paper. Take two squares measuring about four inches and in contrasting colours. Cut parallel slits about half an inch apart in the squares as shown in fig. 2, but leave a small border along one edge of each square to hold the strips together. Stick the squares down on to a card background by the uncut edge, one on top of the other (fig. 3). Once the squares are anchored it is easy to interlace them, working from the top to the bottom.

Several different ideas can be tried using the simple plain weave (fig. 4). Try cutting the strips of different widths and interweaving them; or cut one set of strips in a radiating pattern, leaving the other set straight. Don't feel that you have to work with straight strips; you can cut each square into wavy strips and interweave them.

Fig. 1   The warp and the weft

Fig. 2   How to cut paper for weaving

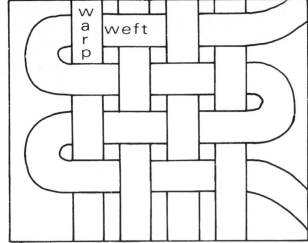

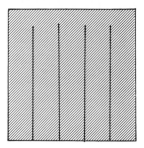

Fig. 3   Positioning paper for weaving

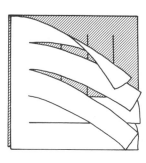

Fig. 4   Black and white woven paper samples

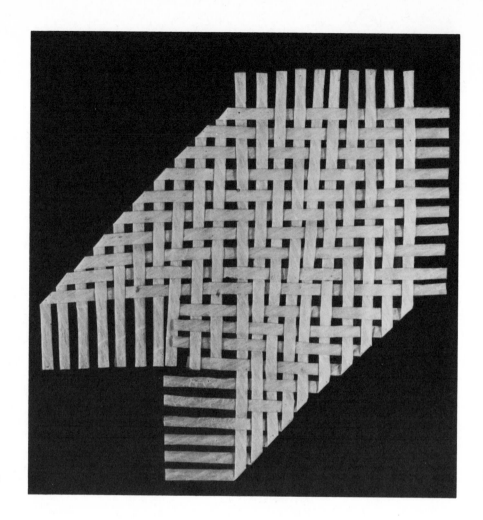

Fig. 5 Woven drinking straws mounted on card

Weaving with drinking straws

Drinking straws can produce some effective patterns. Fig. 5 shows plain drinking straws woven in a plain weave, which has produced, quite accidentally, a strange optical effect. Fig. 6 shows drinking straws that have been covered with silver foil and linked together to produce an idea for an attractive wall decoration. Try combining cut strips of corrugated cardboard with straws; the straws fit nicely into the corrugations. In fig. 7 the woven example has been sprayed with silver paint, which unifies the whole design. Strips of corrugated cardboard can also be woven together (fig. 8). This idea, reproduced on a larger scale, would look effective as a section in a walled area, for example within a recess in a room or on a chimney-breast.

By now you should feel fairly proficient in working in plain weave, so why not venture into twill weaving?

Fig. 6   Drinking straws
covered in foil

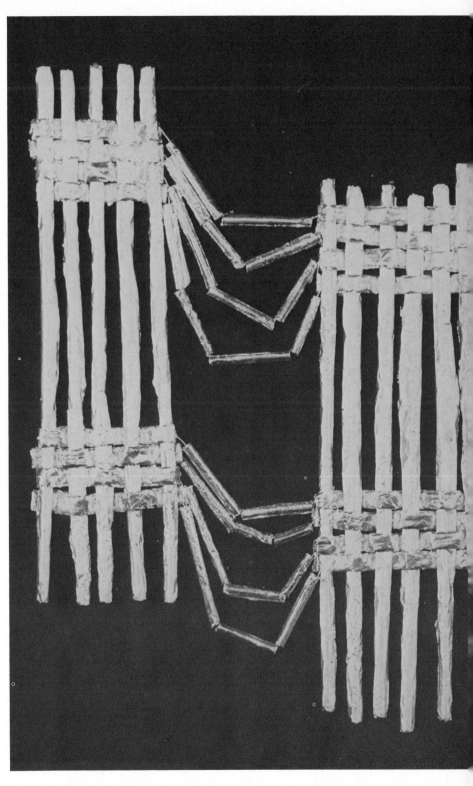

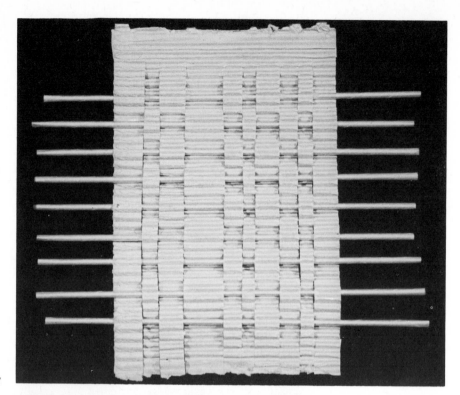

Fig. 7 Drinking straws woven with corrugated card

Fig. 8 Corrugated card strips woven together

Twill weaving

This type of weaving is slightly more complex. Instead of working over two rows, the complete repeat of the pattern works over the four rows (fig. 9).

If we take the first weft row as (A) it will pass over warp threads 1 and 2, then under threads 3 and 4, repeating in this manner across the warp threads. The second weft row (B) will pass under 1, then over 2 and 3, and under 4, repeating across the threads in this way. The third weft row (C) will pass under 1 and 2 and over 3 and 4, repeating across the row. The fourth weft row (D) will pass across 1, under 2 and 3, and across 4, repeating across the row.

These four rows form one repeat of the pattern and can be repeated indenfinitely. It can be seen quite clearly that a horizontal shift of one warp thread is made on each row, and it is this which gives twill its distinctive diagonal effect. It is twill that is used to create so many attractive tartans and tweeds.

How to begin twill weaving

Begin with the sticky paper that was used to demonstrate plain weaving. You may wish to write the numbers that represent the warp strips and the letters that represent the weft strips on to the sticky paper so that you can follow the instructions given above (fig. 9).

Many of the basic patterns in cloth-weaving are based on the twill weave. Once you have mastered the principle of the twill you will be able to experiment with colour to produce a dog's tooth check and herringbone stripe.

Fig. 9   Twill weaving

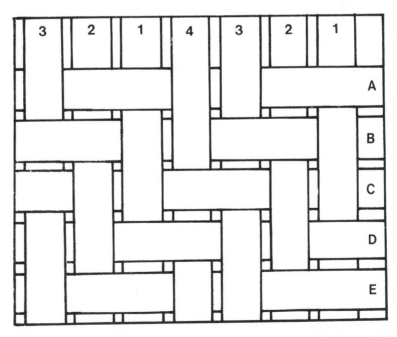

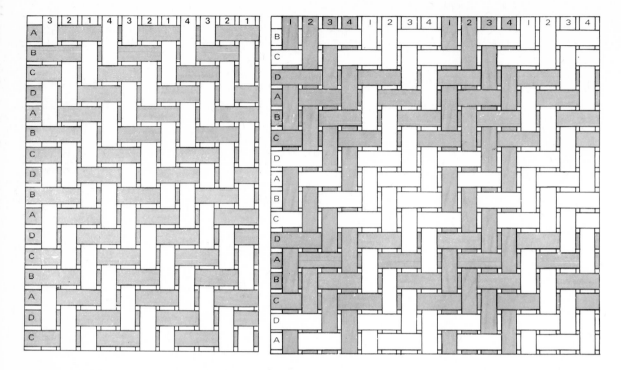

The herringbone stripe

The herringbone stripe is shown in fig. 10. It is worked across four warp strips and down sixteen weft strips. Each strip has been lettered or numbered to aid clarity, and by marking the strips you may find working the pattern easier to start with. All the warp strips are in one colour and the weft strips in a contrasting shade. Basically, the herringbone pattern is a series of twill stripes in one direction. In the diagram it is eight, but you can have any number. The twill stripe is reversed at intervals to give the distinctive design. This reversing is not completely straightforward because between each reversal two weft strips are left out. By leaving the strips out a crisp cut-off line is produced between each set of diagonal stripes. If the two strips are left in the weaving a zigzag effect is obtained. Try both methods and see the effect for yourself.

The dog's tooth check

The weave of this pattern is still based on the twill weave, but the effect is obtained entirely by the use of colour (fig. 11). The warp strips are numbered 1 to 4—one block in one colour and the second block in a contrasting colour—and so on, alternating the blocks across the warp. The weft strips are arranged similarly in blocks of four strips to each colour. The weft strips are labelled A B C D and the pattern is shown beginning with C.

To begin the pattern

> *Row 1.* Take weft C over warp 1, under warps 2 and 3, and over 4; continue across the warp in this way.
> *Row 2.* Weft D over warps 1 and 2 and under warps 3 and 4, continuing across the warp.
> *Row 3.* Weft A under warp 1, over 2 and 3, and under 4, continuing in pattern.
> *Row 4.* Weft B under warps 1 and 2, and over 3 and 4 continuing in pattern.

The above four rows complete the pattern and can be repeated indefinitely.

Working with colour

Colour, as you will have now begun to realize, is one of the most important aspects of weaving. Colour is also one of the most difficult things to visualize, mainly because as soon as you place two colours side by side they visually affect one another.

Here is one of the most well-used colour experiments in art colleges. Take three coloured squares of paper and cut them to measure 2 in. × 2 in. The following colours show the effect best: bright red, yellow and mid blue. Using a piece of mid-grey paper, cut three squares measuring $\frac{1}{2}$ in. × $\frac{1}{2}$ in. and stick each one in the centre of one of the coloured squares. Place the three squares on a white background. You should be able to see an interesting effect, which is that each grey appears to be a different grey from its neighbour. The effect is caused by the colour surrounding the grey, so although you know that each grey is the same, your eyes are tricked into seeing them as different shades of grey. Remember that all colours affect each other, and this is why it is difficult to visualize the final effect of one particular colour in a piece of work.

When planning a colour scheme, don't always use 'safe' colours. If you experiment first with strips of coloured tissue paper you will find, because of the transparency of tissue, that new colours occur where two colours cross one another; these new colours may work better than the ones you had originally decided to use. One other way of experimenting in a semi-accidental way with colour is to take two photographs from a magazine and cut them into strips ready for weaving. Use one for the warp and one for the weft and interweave them. You will be surprised and fascinated by the results you obtain (fig. 12).

Colour schemes

The 'safe' colours (that is those which will 'go' together) in my terminology are those which are neighbours on the colour wheel (fig. 13), e.g. blue, blue/violet, and violet; or red, orange and yellow. Other safe colours include the neutrals—the beiges, greys, off-whites—which I tend to think of as

Fig. 12 Woven photographs

Fig. 13 The colour wheel

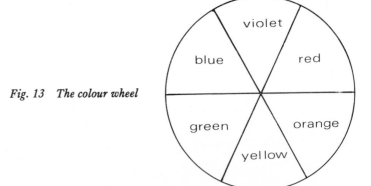

Scandinavian colours. The muted colours include earthy shades like red-ochre, yellow-ochre, brown, khaki and rust. Pastel colours are any of the colours already mentioned but made lighter in tone by the addition of white.

Devising your own colour schemes

There are different ways of devising colour schemes, but a little basic knowledge about colour theory always helps. Red, yellow and blue are the primary colours. By mixing red and yellow you produce orange; yellow and blue make green; and red and blue should make violet, but if your red is too orangey the resulting colour may be brown.

Using colour in a warp and weft

Using this knowledge of colour mixing you could use, for example, a red warp and a yellow weft to obtain an orange fabric, and the colour would be far more vibrant than if a plain orange warp and weft had been used. 'Shot silk' obtains its effect by using warp and weft in this way. Because you can mix two different colours to produce another colour, very subtle colours can be developed. For example, by using a cerise warp with an orange weft a really rich red can be obtained. You are not, of course, confined to using only one colour in either warp or weft but mixed designs are dealt with in later chapters.

Complementary colours

Some colours, when used together, will give a dazzling effect. Painters favouring optical painting use this knowledge to their advantage. These colours are called complementary and they are found opposite one another across the colour wheel. Thus red and green, blue and orange, and violet and yellow are complementary, and so are all the shades in between—turquoise and orangey red, bluish violet and orangey yellow, and so on. Try using pairs of complementary colours within a paper-weaving scheme, perhaps in designs of stripes or tartans. Begin to think in terms of designing in colour from the results of your earlier experiments.

Planning a design

First it is necessary to decide what design is. Basically, it is the ability to express your ideas in a concrete way, but there are many variables to be taken into consideration. In weaving, the first thing to consider is the design of the weave. Some simple examples to give you ideas are given in this chapter. Next comes the use of colour, and thirdly the use of materials (a subject which we will be considering throughout the book). The fourth and last variable is that amorphous 'something' which is actually the production of a vague idea by using and integrating the three previous mentioned variables. So often the idea in your head just doesn't work when translated into a piece of weaving. But along the path of experiment you may well develop an even better idea, so don't be discouraged. Two things to remember are that you can weave with literally anything, *and* that your end-product does not necessarily have to be flat. Fig. 14 shows a lampshade developed from the sample ideas shown in fig. 4, and fig. 15 shows a waste-paper basket actually woven from waste paper! The construction of the basket was started flat, with warp and weft lengths extending out from a square, woven base. These lengths were then bent up to form the sides of the basket and further lengths were woven around the circumference of the basket until the walls were the required height. The lengths used to make the basket were made of flattened rolls of newspaper.

Fig. 14   Woven paper lampshade

*Fig. 15 Newspaper
waste-paper basket*

2 Yarns, dyeing, and weaving into and on to fabrics

With the introduction of fabrics we now begin to use yarns. The word yarn is used instead of thread, wool or cord because it is a collective term used to describe all kinds of threads and fibres. There are many types of yarn which differ not only in composition, but also in thickness and shape.

The natural fibres

The natural fibres are those obtained from natural sources and these sources can be subdivided into animal, vegetable and mineral.

Animal fibres

Of the animal fibres the most common is wool, obtained from the fleece of sheep. There are several specialized wool fibres like cashmere, vicuna, camel and llama hair but the only one that you are likely to use, apart from wool, is mohair. Mohair is obtained from the long-haired angora goat. Another small animal (using animal in its widest sense) to whom we are indebted is the silk moth for the production of silk.

Vegetable fibres

The vegetable fibres are obtained from various plants. Cotton comes from the pod or boll of the cotton plant. Linen originates from the fibrous stalks of flax plants and jute from the stalk of the jute plant. Hemp is also a vegetable fibre and there are several varieties of hemp plant which produce this fibre.

Mineral fibres

These are obtained, as the name suggests, from mineral sources. Asbestos is very useful as a flame retardant and insulator, but due to the irritant nature of the fibres it is highly unlikely that you will use it. Glass fibre, which is produced from a fine glass thread or filament, makes up into fabrics suitable for curtains and it too has insulating properties. Glass fibre is not suitable for clothing fabrics as small splinters may rub off the fabric and cause irritation. Metallic fibres are not normally used alone but are often wound with a strengthening cotton core or else plastic coated. Even with these methods of strengthening, the metallic thread is brittle by comparison with other fibres.

Synthetic fibres

Synthetic fibres are now a large group and are produced from a wide range of raw materials, from cellulose to petrol and coal. Rayon, of which there are several varieties, derives from cellulose. Acetates originate from cellulose acetate. Other synthetic fibres include the acrylics, the polyesters and the nylons.

The shape of yarns

Having discussed very briefly the composition of yarns, it is now necessary to look into the thickness and shape of yarns. Most yarns can be spun to produce curls and loops, like mohair loop wool. Lumps, either regular or irregular, rather like bouclé, can be produced along the length of a yarn and extra bits can be added like slubs. Several colours can be wound together and various types of yarn can be combined to produce, for example, a Terylene and cotton mixture.

Yarn counts

When buying knitting wool you will have noticed that yarn is supplied in different plys. In weaving, yarns are numbered in a similar way to denote both thickness and ply. If you have to buy yarn you will see it is numbered, for example '3/12s'. This denotes a three-ply yarn with a thickness of twelve, which is quite fine. '2/1' is a two-ply yarn with a thickness of one, which is very thick. The lower the number the thicker the thread. The ply number is always placed in front of the thickness number.

Dyeing yarns

Many yarns are produced in a limited colour range and it is always useful to know how to change the yarn to the colour you require. Man-made fibres like nylon do not usually dye to dark shades. Wool, cotton and silk will usually 'take up' different shades of the same dye. Different types of yarn treated with exactly the same dye can produce completely different colours. If you buy a household dye normally there are instructions included which, if followed correctly, will produce the required colour.

Equipment

The basic equipment you will require is as follows:

1. A dye container, large enough to contain your yarn and allow for easy manipulation and complete coverage of the yarn by the dye liquor. The container should be heat-proof unless you are using a cold-water dye.
2. A small metal container for heating and dissolving the dye before it is added to the dye-bath.
3. A wooden spoon for stirring the yarn in the dye-bath.
4. A bowl or sink for rinsing and damping down the yarn.
5. Salt. Most dye recipes require salt.
6. A gas ring or an electric hot plate for heating the dye-bath.
7. Spin-dryer. This is optional, but it is a useful extra and considerably shortens yarn-drying time.

Preparing the yarn for dyeing

To prepare any yarn for dyeing it is necessary to wind it into skeins. You should never attempt to dye a ball of yarn because it is very difficult to get complete penetration of dye to the centre of the ball. To make a skein, place two chairs back to back and wind the yarn around the backs of the chairs. Another method is to use hands supported at the elbows on a table or similar surface (fig. 16). Do not make the skein too thick. To prevent the skein becoming tangled during dyeing, place several stay-cords, of a contrasting colour, in the skein (fig. 17). These stay-cords are looped through the skein in a figure of eight. They *must not* be tied too tightly or they will produce a tie dye effect, with some dyed and some undyed areas. This effect, although attractive, is very irritating if you wanted a solid colour. If you are dyeing a yarn that is excessively greasy, you should first wash the skein in a liquid grease-removing detergent. This will allow greater dye penetration. It is advisable to follow the dyeing instructions included with your particular dye, as methods vary with different brands. When the skeins have dried, place them on the chair backs again, remove the stay-cords and rewind the yarn into balls.

Using your yarns

In the first chapter, the two basic weaves were introduced, and it was shown how colour could be used to produce apparent variations in the weaves. You can now work these weaves into a fabric. For practice purposes use a loosely woven fabric like hessian or linen for your first experiments. If you have a circular embroidery frame you will find your fabric easier to handle when it is stretched taut. You can also use a square embroidery frame, sometimes obtainable with legs which means you can work on a supported surface. If you

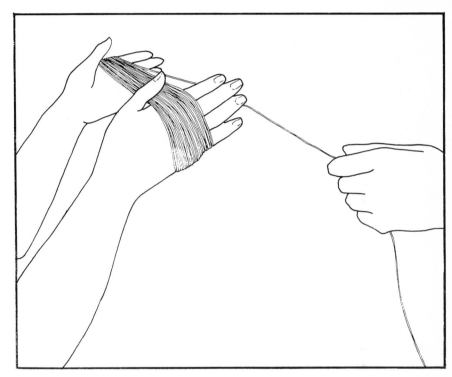

Fig. 16   A skein of yarn

Fig. 17   Stay-cords in position through a skein of yarn

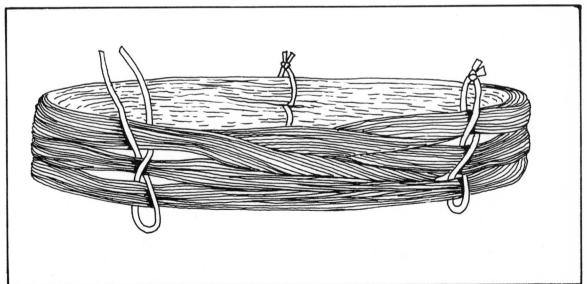

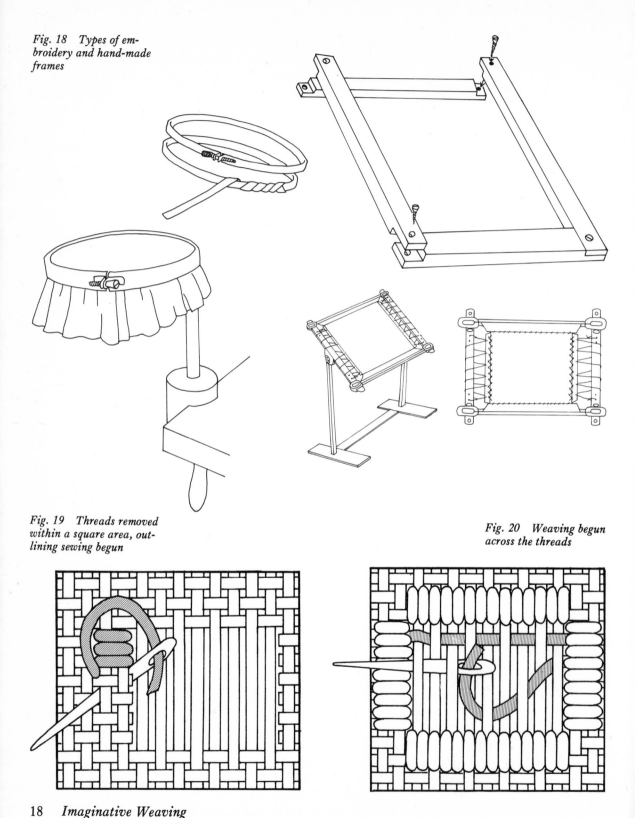

Fig. 18   Types of embroidery and hand-made frames

Fig. 19   Threads removed within a square area, outlining sewing begun

Fig. 20   Weaving begun across the threads

do not want the expense of buying a square frame it is easy to make your own, using four lengths of wood screwed together, as shown in fig. 18.

If you have ever attempted drawn-thread work in embroidery the technique of weaving into a fabric will immediately be clearer to you.

Working into a fabric

Begin by stretching your sample piece of fabric on to its frame. If you are using an embroidery hoop, a better tension can be obtained by first binding the inner hoop with tape before stretching the fabric. Begin working on a section approximately one inch square. Remove all the threads in one direction (fig. 19) within the one-inch area. To prevent fraying of the fabric, oversew around the edge of the square with thick wool or cotton. Start with plain weaving. Use a large-eyed, semi-blunt needle, similar to the type used to sew up knitted garments, and thread up with a thick wool in a contrasting colour. Begin by working backwards and forwards across the square, passing the needle through the oversewn edge at each end (fig. 20). Continue in this way until you have filled up the square. Now experiment with different yarns. Try a mohair loop type of yarn and a bouclé or similar lumpy yarn, and notice how you obtain different fabric effects with them. Now repeat the experiment with twill weaving. Try and link up the various squares that you have worked by adding squares in between. Think of other methods of filling for the squares. Some ideas are shown in figs 21, 22, 23 and 24.

Using unusual materials

Once you have experimented with ordinary yarns, think of what other materials could be threaded through fabric to create different textures. The example in fig. 25 shows velvet ribbon and sequins.

Fig. 21 Leno effect in needleweaving

Fig. 22   Gathering bunches in needleweaving

Fig. 23   Woven blocks in needleweaving

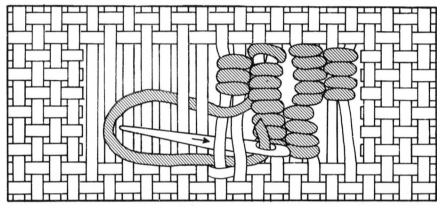

Fig. 24   A hessian wall hanging

Fig. 25   Drawn-thread work with sequins and velvet ribbon

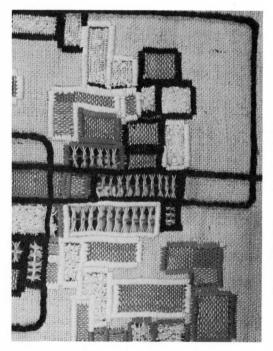

Working within shaped areas

So far, we have worked only in square shapes. It is now time to try more adventurous designs. If you want to produce a circle, merely draw it lightly on to the back of your fabric and remove a set of threads in whichever direction you wish, keeping within the drawn shape (fig. 26). The shape can be oversewn in a similar way to the squares to produce a decorative edge or, using a fine cotton in a colour matching the fabric, can be oversewn almost invisibly. Threads can be removed in either direction and in some cases in both directions. If you remove every other thread in both warp and weft, the result will be two sets of threads lying one on top of the other not not interlacing (fig. 27). This means that two layers of interweaving can be attempted or alternatively, a double-sided fabric can be worked.

To make two chokers

Using the idea of removing threads within a shaped area some interesting ideas can be developed, and two of these are shown in fig. 28. The two patterns for the chokers (figs. 29 and 30) are designed to fit an average neck but they are adjustable.

Fig. 26 Removing threads within a circular area

Fig. 27 Removing threads within both warp and weft

The 'eye' choker

Begin with the pattern for the eye. Each square equals a quarter of an inch, so

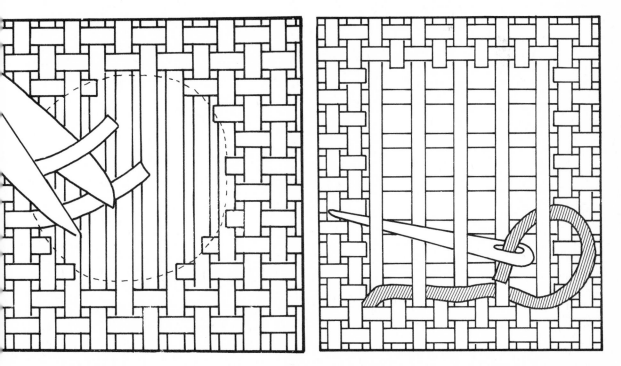

to work from the pattern you will need some graph paper with quarter-inch squares. Transfer the outline on to your graph paper which is used as a pattern for cutting around the fabric. Using a medium-weight cotton or linen fabric, trace the design lightly on to the back of the fabric, and stretch in an embroidery frame.

Remove all the horizontal threads within the two shaded crescent areas, leaving the shorter vertical threads in position. Oversew in satin-stitch completely around the eye shape and also across the centre strip left between the crescent shapes. If you are working on a fairly fine material and the embroidery silk you are using is of a coarser thickness than the threads of the fabric, it may be easier to pass your needle over and under pairs of threads

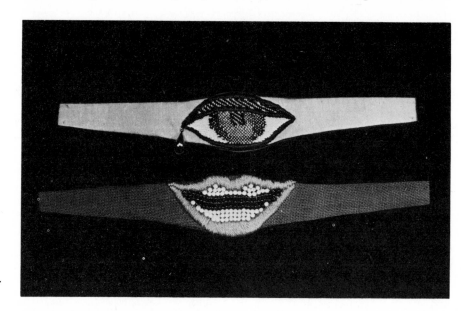

Fig. 28   Two chokers incorporating weaving (see colour plate opposite page 56).

Fig. 29   Grid pattern for the eye choker.

Fig. 30   Grid pattern for the mouth choker

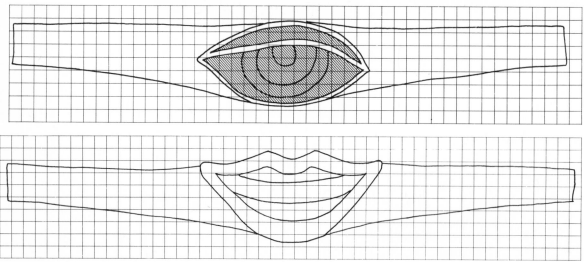

rather than single threads to produce a plain, even-weave fabric (fig. 31).

Begin by weaving on the section equivalent to the white of the eye. When the weaving reaches the oversewn edge, pass it through the edge to give a firmer piece of weaving. Work the iris of the eye in the same way. When the weaving thread reaches the woven edge of the white of the eye, pass the thread through the loop formed at the edge of the weaving, thus linking them together. The pupil and the lid of the eye are worked similarly, but instead of a plain weave a twill weave has been used. To finish the design I added a pearlized tear-drop bead at the corner of the eye. This of course is optional. To complete the choker, turn in all the edges and tack them. Cut out a lining of a similar material slightly larger than the original pattern and turn

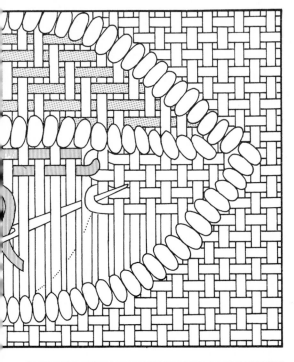

Fig. 31   Weaving method used in the eye choker

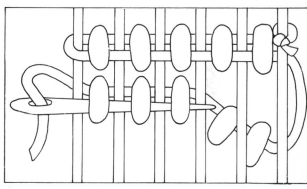

Fig. 32   Bead weaving used for the mouth choker

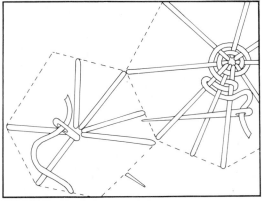

Fig. 33   Beginning radiating surface weaving

Yarns, dyeing, and weaving into and on to fabrics   23

in the edges and tack them. Pin both raw-edge surfaces together and hem them. Remove all tacking stitches and sew a length of ribbon to each end of the choker for fastening purposes.

The 'mouth' choker

To make the mouth choker, begin in a similar way to the eye. Transfer the pattern on to the fabric and outline the lips in satin-stitch. I used a thick cotton for the embroidery as the fabric I used was quite a loose weave. In my pattern the inside of the mouth and the teeth are worked completely in beads, but these areas could be needle-woven in a similar way to the eye if preferred. Withdraw all the horizontal threads from the fabric within the mouth shape, leaving only the vertical threads. Ideally, the beads you use should be the same size as the spaces between the vertical threads. Mine, in fact, were twice this size and this necessitated removing every other vertical thread to allow room for the beads. I have drawn an explanatory diagram (fig. 32) which I hope will demonstrate the technique of bead weaving. Bead weaving on a loom can be seen in chapter 6.

Bead weaving Fig. 32 shows the back of the work. First count the number of spaces between the threads that you have within the working area. Anchor your thread on an outside edge and thread up with the same number of beads as you have spaces. Tighten your thread until the beads have worked back to the anchor point. Now slacken the thread slightly and allow a bead to drop into each space with a vertical thread in between. Take up your needle and place it behind the work. Push each bead down singly and pass the needle through it once more. This second thread should be passing under the vertical threads and thus anchoring the beads in position. These instructions explain the basic technique of bead weaving. Within the shaped area of the mouth it is necessary to have different numbers of beads on each row but otherwise the technique is the same. To finish the choker refer to the finishing instructions for the 'eye' design. Bead weaving is described in more detail on page 90.

Surface needleweaving

So far our weaving has worked into the existing threads of the fabric. It is, however, quite feasible to create your own threads on the surface of a fabric and needleweave with these as the colour plate opposite page 40 demonstrates. Fig. 33 shows the method for beginning radiating weaving. Start by stitching radiating threads, like the spokes of a wheel. Always stitch an uneven number of threads; you will then be able to use these threads to interweave in a circle like the base of a wicker basket. The whole area can be filled with the circular design or you can weave individual branches; the choice is yours.

Insertions and edgings

Other ways of using needleweaving are by insertions and edgings. I have shown, with the aid of diagrams and photographs, two simple designs.

Working the insertion

The two fabric edges that form the basic edges for the insertion must first be hemmed to prevent fraying (fig. 34). Tack the fabric on to a stiff backing with the two hemmed edges approximately half an inch apart. Work a zig-zag foundation thread as shown in the diagram. Then interweave between the threads forming each triangular shape (fig. 35). Insertions can be used at any place where a seam would normally be worked, making allowance for the fact that the insertion adds half an inch to any seam that it is applied to.

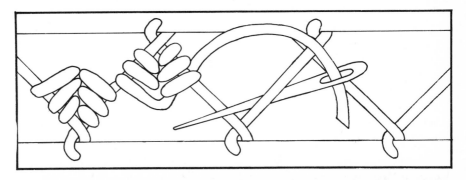

Fig. 34 Working the insertion

Fig. 35 Insertion needleweaving

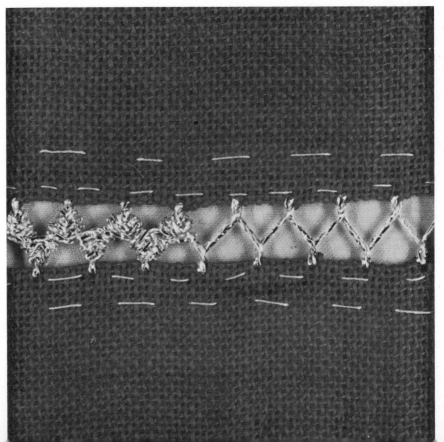

Working the edging

Edgings can be worked on to necklines, armholes, jacket fronts and so on. The edge must be finished either by binding, backing or facing and then tacked on to a cardboard background. Draw in pencil on the card the intended position of the decorative scallops. Outline the pencil shape with small back-stitches, using ordinary sewing cotton. Using embroidery thread, begin at the centre of the scallop, work a series of radiating threads which pass through the back stitches on the surface of the card (fig. 36). Take up a small piece of fabric at the centre position on each radiating stitch that is sewn. The idea is then to interweave in a half circle across these radiating stitches, taking up a small piece of fabric at each side to secure the half circle to the fabric edge. Continue weaving until the radiating stitches are completely filled, then begin work on the adjacent scallop. Once the scallops have been worked, the card backing can be removed.

Fig. 36   Working a scalloped edge

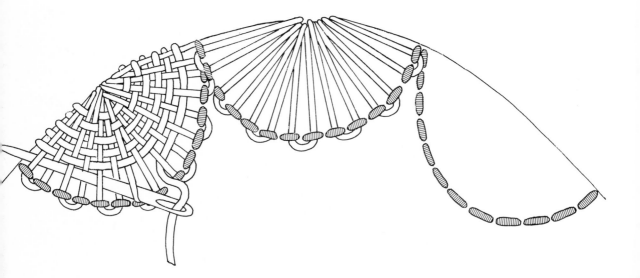

3 Card weaving

With all the ideas shown in this book it is advisable to begin in a simple way and develop through experiment. One of the simplest looms to work on is constructed from thick cardboard; the diagrams here show several methods of making such looms. In the illustrations they are shown square, but one of the best reasons for making a cardboard loom is that all kinds of shapes can be worked, which would not be possible on a normal hand loom.

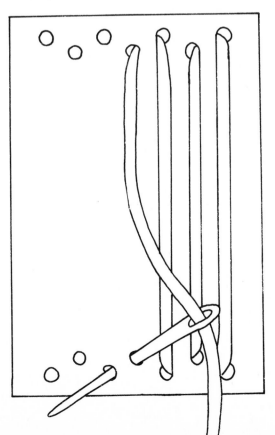

Fig. 38   Card loom with holes to hold warp thread

Making card looms

Fig. 38 shows the method of securing the warp threads by making holes in the card. The easiest way to do this is by threading a large-eyed needle with your warp thread and pushing it through your card, as shown. You may have to start the holes with a pair of scissors.

Fig. 39 shows notches cut into the card edge to hold the warp thread. You can also make slits in the edge of a card. Fig. 40 shows pins placed in the card along two opposite edges. With this method, the warp thread can either be wound round each pin head or around two pins, which is useful if you are working with a thick yarn or if you want to vary the spaces between your warp threads.

You may feel that card is restricting as a medium, but you are not obliged to use only card; there are many other materials available which are probably better. For example, a plastic tea tray can make an excellent flat loom and it is easy to cut slots at the edges to take warp threads. Expanded polystyrene and pins will also make a firm basis for weaving. So try out other likely materials as you go.

Solving basic problems

When using these looms you will encounter certain basic problems. For

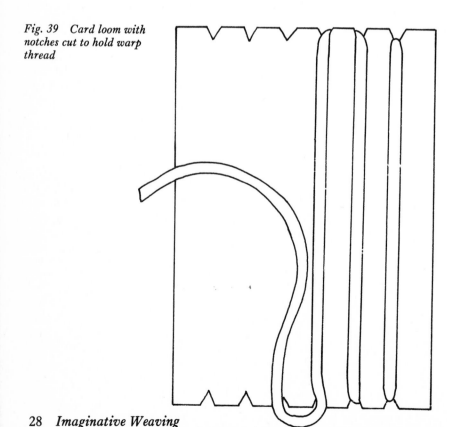

Fig. 39   Card loom with notches cut to hold warp thread

example, how much yarn you will need; what type of yarn you should use; what the purpose is of the finished article; what working methods you should employ, and so on.

Calculating the length of warp yarn needed

This is fairly simple. Measure the length of your card (that is the way the warp will lie); let us say it is six inches. Prepare your card for weaving, using one of the methods already described. Once you have made the required number of slits or notches, with reference to the diagrams, work out how many times your thread will pass along the length of your card. In our example it will be twenty-four times. Multiply twenty-four by six (inches) and then add twice the width for wastage, say four inches, to the total. If you are now completely confused, refer to the calculation set out below! Your calculation should look like this:

$$24 \times 6 = 144 + 8 = 152 \text{ inches.}$$

By substituting your own measurements for these sample ones, you will be able to calculate how much warp yarn you will need. I usually add another twelve inches, which will probably be wastage, because your yarn generally stretches as it comes under tension.

Fig. 40   Card loom with pins in the edge to hold warp thread

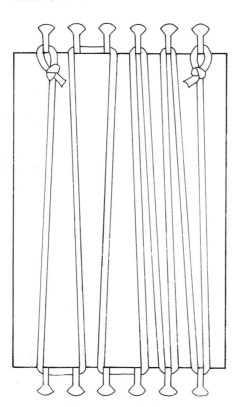

How to fasten the warp ends

To fasten each warp end, either knot so that the knot lies snug in the first and last slots, or knot around the beginning and ending pins (fig. 41).

Type of yarn to use

The type of yarn is more difficult to choose for several reasons. The easiest yarn to work with is a thick cotton, which will not stretch too much, but this could be harsh to the touch. The most difficult yarn to deal with is a thin wool because it is stretchy, liable to break, and fluffs up as it is worked. To begin your piece of weaving, use either a two-ply rug yarn or a medium-weight knitting or crochet cotton. If you are designing your work for a specific purpose, think . . . is it to be hung, worn, used frequently or kept purely as a decorative piece? If it is just a sample, don't worry at this stage about usage. For a table of types of yarn and their uses see page 118.

Working methods

Decide on which yarn to use and wind the necessary amount on to your card loom, fastening it with a knot at each end. You will need to use a shuttle to hold your weft yarn.

Making a shuttle

Take a rectangle of thick card, measuring one inch by about two and a half inches. Mark out an outline on it, following the dotted line shown in fig. 42. Cut through the card along the dotted line. Remove the shaded areas of card, and the remaining piece forms your shuttle. A darning needle can be used instead of a shuttle for small areas. Yarn is wound around the shuttle passing through the slits at the top and bottom.

Fig. 41   Starting to weave

Fig. 42   Making a card shuttle

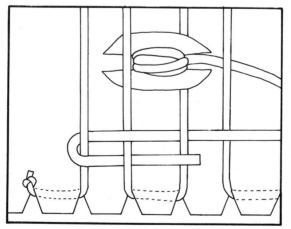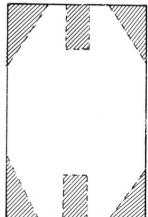

To begin weaving

Unwind about twelve inches of weft yarn from your shuttle. Interweave your shuttle through the base of the warp threads in a plain weave pattern. Leave a two-inch free end at the beginning. Before working back for a second row, interweave the two-inch free end around the outermost warp thread and then back into the weaving (fig. 41). This creates a neat edge and the free end is covered by succeeding rows of weaving. Remember it is easier to start at the bottom of a cardboard loom and work upwards; it is always tempting to work from the top to the bottom.

Joining in extra yarn

You will not be able to wind enough yarn on your shuttle to complete the whole piece of weaving, so it will be necessary to join in fresh yarn. The method of joining is shown in fig. 43. Allow your yarn to run out, then join in a new length overlapping the previous length by about two inches. Any odd ends that are left can be removed with scissors when the weaving is completed. To make the join firm, continue weaving and the successive rows (or picks as they are called in weaving) will secure the join.

Some tips on successful weaving

Do not pull your weft yarn too tight as this will cause the weaving to tighten up and your outer edges or selvedges will begin to bow inwards giving an uneven edge.

Do try and keep your weaving even. After each row use the shuttle, a ruler or a large-toothed comb to push down on the weft. This will make the yarn interweave correctly between the warp threads. Fig. 44 shows the view through the weaving if you could cut through the warp threads and look down on them. (A) shows the weft yarn pulled too tight; (B) shows how it

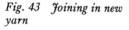

Fig. 43 Joining in new yarn

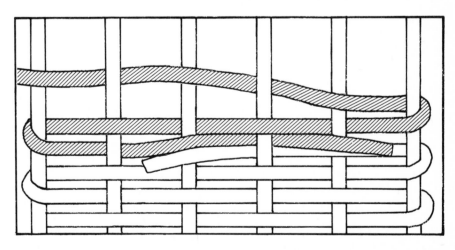

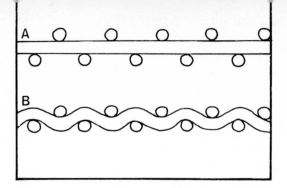

Fig. 44 *Two views showing correct and incorrect weaving*

Fig. 45 *Making an arc in the weft yarn*

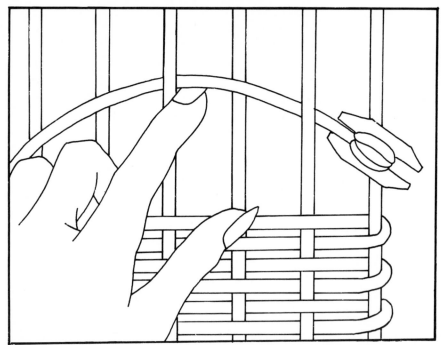

should interlace between the warp threads. Sometimes to get this degree of looseness in the weft thread, as you weave you can form an arc shape. The method of making an arc on each pick is to use your finger to support the weft after the shuttle has passed through the warp. Fig. 45 demonstrates this technique. The arc of weft yarn is pushed down the warp to interweave with the main weaving.

Circular card-loom weaving

Once you have worked with a square card loom, you can go on to try the circular flat card loom which introduces further possibilities.

Making a circular card loom

Using a compass, mark out a circle measuring about four iches across. Cut out this circle, then, using a ruler, draw a line across the circle making sure it passes through the centre point. From this straight line draw a series of radiating lines from the centre point to the rim of the circle. These lines must add up to an *uneven* number; you will see why when you begin weaving. Treat the rim of the circle in the same way as the edge of the cardboard square loom and either slit, notch or slide in pins around the edge of the circle, following your radiating pencil lines for the correct positioning.

Weaving on a circular loom

Begin at the outer edge by fastening your thread with a knot. Then pass your thread across the circle to the opposite side (fig. 46). Continue working backwards and forwards across the circle in this way until all the slits are filled. When you have filled your last slot, bring your yarn back to the centre and begin to interweave between the radiating threads in a circular motion. At this stage you will see why it was necessary to have an odd number of threads: once you have completed one circular movement to get the correct weaving there must be one extra radiating thread to make the weaving in-

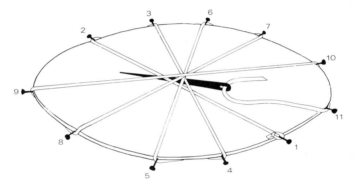

Fig. 46   Making a circular card loom

terlace in the correct way. Continue working round the circle until you have filled the radiating threads with weaving. *Do not* pull the outermost circles of weaving too tight, or these will tighten up when the weaving is removed from the loom and the centre of the weaving will bulge outwards. Any odd ends should be worked back into the weaving using a darning needle. Fig. 47 shows some ideas for things to make from your circles of weaving. Not only can you make garments, rugs, and tablecloths, but also small items like belts, place mats, bags, pan holders and wallhangings. The circles can be joined by oversewing at the points where two edges meet.

Further ideas

Once you have developed a degree of skill in producing plain weaving circles, try other weaving patterns such as twill. Another pattern is shown in fig. 48. This involves winding the weft thread around each radiating thread individually to produce a ribbed effect. This pattern can also be used to in-

Fig. 47   Some design ideas for circular card weaving

Fig. 48   Weaving ridges in circular card weaving

Fig. 49   Introducing beads into circular card weaving

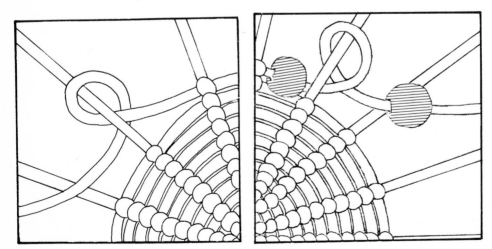

34   *Imaginative Weaving*

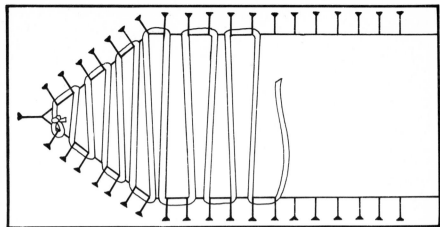

introduce beads to decorate the flat areas between the radiating ridges (fig. 49). Remember to thread the beads on to the weft thread before starting to weave, unless you are using a needle to weave with, when beads can be threaded on as you proceed. Fig. 50 shows some body jewellery woven on a circular loom.

To obtain a lacy effect, instead of working continuously around in circles, work backwards and forwards to form a block of weaving within an area, rather like surface needleweaving (fig. 33). Leave some areas unwoven.

Other shapes

You are not of course restricted to making card shapes with just squares and circles. Small items like watch straps can also be set up on a card loom. You will probably find that the pointed end of the watch strap will need strengthening by oversewing or glueing on the reverse side to prevent the movement of the weaving (fig. 51). Mule-type slippers are another item that can be produced on a card loom. The uppers are usually woven while the soles can be of plaited raffia, hide or foam rubber. It is possible to buy commercially produced cards that are already marked out for making slippers. You will see here a pattern for making the uppers of a pair of slippers in leather using an entirely new interlacing pattern as an alternative to a bought pattern.

Working a pair of slippers

Fig. 52 shows a grid pattern with equally spaced squares. To enlarge the pattern to your requirements take a sheet of paper and mark it out in a grid of larger squares, with the same number of squares as shown in the pattern. It is simple to transfer the pattern to your grid; just note where each pattern line crosses a grid line and draw this in to complete an outline of the upper. The pattern shown is for the right foot; to produce a left foot just reverse the

Fig. 50   Body jewellery

Fig. 51   Making a watch strap

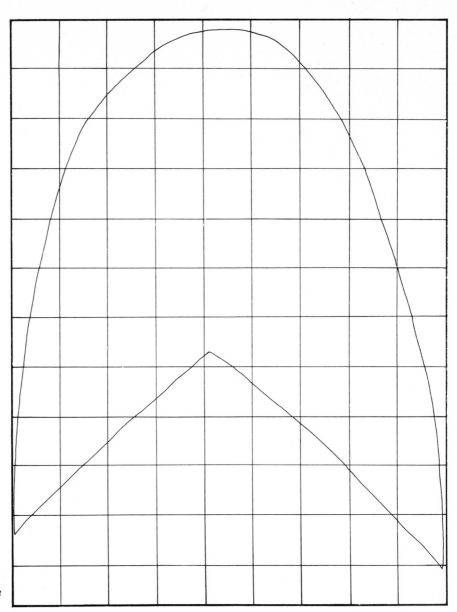

Fig. 52   Grid pattern for a
pair of leather slippers

pattern. One-inch squares will produce slippers to fit a $5\frac{1}{2}$–6 size foot. Fig. 53
shows the pattern of interlacing. Each leather strip is half an inch wide. It will
be easier to follow if a rough design is drawn on to your pattern. The
easiest way to work is with the pattern pinned to a twelve-inch square, thick
polystyrene block. The leather can then be positioned more easily. One last
tip: use a multi-purpose glue to hold all the interlacing strips at the outer
edges. The slippers are mounted on a thick, foam-rubber sole, covered with
leather. Get the sole shape by drawing round your own foot.

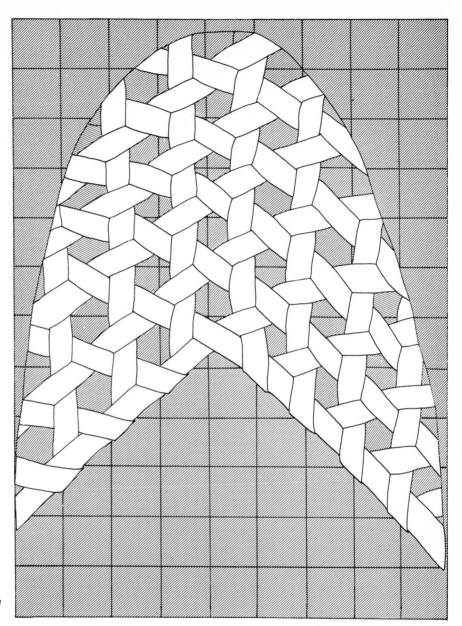

Fig. 53 Interlacing for the leather slippers

Making garments on shaped boards

Larger garments can be worked in a similar way to the small items but it is better to work these on a board with nails or panel pins, rather than card (fig. 54). Polystyrene of sufficient thickness (at least two inches) can be shaped and used for supporting garments in this way. The type of garments that can be worked on a board are waistcoat-type jackets, bikinis, boleros, kaftan trimmings, and various accessories like collars, cuffs and berets. Always remember to keep garment shapes very simple.

Working from a paper design

So far weaving has been developed as a straightforward building up of fabric row by row or (to describe it correctly) pick by pick. Among your first experiments you will have made squares and circles of weaving and tried different yarns and colours, but as yet no reference has been made towards translating a paper design into weaving or working in a more abstract way with threads.

Using one of your simple card looms, draw a design on its surface. The pattern should be a simple geometric design in two colours. Put a warp on your card in the usual way. Using one colour for your background, commence weaving until your design area is reached. You will now have to decide which tapestry technique you are going to use to work the design. Two methods are shown here and you can decide for yourself which is the most suitable.

Kilim or slit weaving

The technique of slit weaving or kilim, which incidently dates back to at least 2500 B.C., is a method of leaving slits between sections of weaving and often between different areas of colour. When using kilim, your slits should enhance the design. Geometric patterns look good in this technique, but it can look unsightly if used in the wrong design. The simplest form of kilim is shown in fig. 55. There are many variations and these will be introduced in later chapters.

Interlocking

The interlocking technique, shown in fig. 56, can be worked in two ways. In the first method, work your design shape first. Then, using your background colour threaded through a needle rather than a shuttle, fill in the background weaving. Interlock the design shape with the background as you work around it. The second method is to use two shuttles both working together and interlocking as they meet to form the design shape. The latter method is preferable because it is the technique you would use if working on a loom.

Abstract

One last design idea to finish this chapter. Try to imagine a fast-flowing river with areas of foam, eddies and currents; how would you translate this into a woven design. Find a photograph of this type of water, place a piece of tracing paper over the photo and outline in pencil the lines that accentuate the rush of the water. The result may look something like fig. 57. Trace this design on to your card loom. When you are working an abstract design of this type, begin at the centre circle. You will then find that you can build up the flowing outlines more easily.

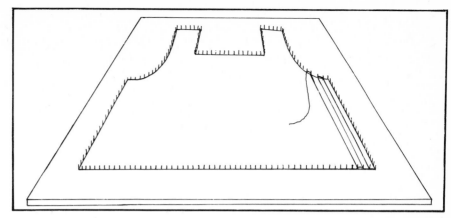

Fig. 54   Working a gar-
ment on a board

Fig. 55   Slit weaving or
kilim

Fig. 56   Interlocking
weaving

Fig. 57   An abstract
design based on the flow of
water

Card weaving   39

4 Working with frames

Weaving frames can be divided into two categories; those frames which remain and form part of the work, and those from which the work is removed so that they can be used again and again. Home-made frames such as that shown in fig. 18 are most likely to become an integral part of the work because by the time you have hammered nails into the frame or wound warp threads around it, it is impossible to remove the weaving anyway.

Frames that become part of the work

This type of frame doesn't have to be a square frame; embroidery hoops make reasonably cheap and hard-wearing circular looms. There is no reason why you can't use a combination of a circular and a square loom in one piece of work. Old adhesive tape reels make very cheap circular looms, and of course wire can be used to shape irregular and abstract shapes. Remember, when using wire, that there is a limit to how large you can make a shape before it begins to distort, but in fact even this distortion can be used to gain a dynamic effect. Much of the first work you produce will owe as much to accident as to design. Plastic tubing can be used either alone for its flexibility or around a wire core to produce a more rigid shape. Once you start looking around you will be amazed by the number of shapes that present themselves to you: curved twigs from a pruned tree, lengths of old tubing, an old deck-chair frame, hoop earrings and bracelets, miscellaneous old picture frames and so on. You will soon become a human magpie, whose favourite haunts are junk shops and attics.

Beginning to work on a frame

Make yourself a simple wooden frame. One kind is shown in fig. 18 or you

Left: *Ribbon weaving using the kilim technique. Note the weft used as the warp.*

Below: *Surface needleweaving combined with weaving into fabric threads.*

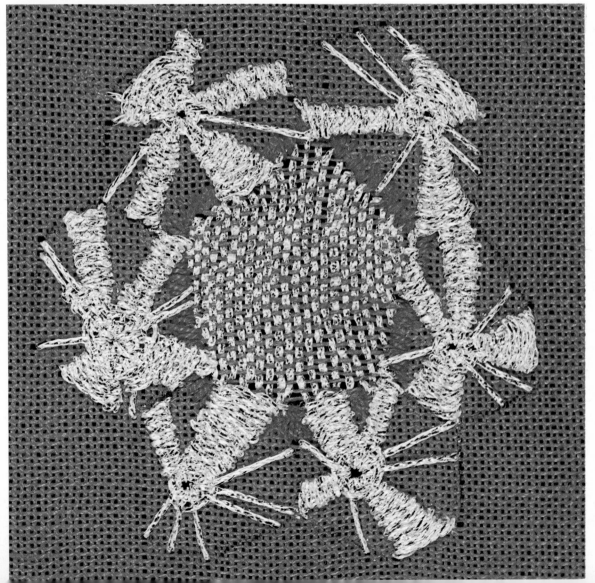

A cross-section of an orange in collage.

could use an old picture frame. Hammer a few nails indiscriminately around the edge of the frame. Try not to let your spacing become too regular. Take up a length of crochet cotton and idly wind it backwards and forwards across the frame, and perhaps from corner to corner too. You will begin to see areas forming within the frame. Fasten off your lengths of crochet cotton and begin to accentuate the thicker areas by interweaving lengths of yarn within these areas only. You could gather a few lengths of the original cotton together and perhaps wrap a separate length around these to give the work different thicknesses. You will begin to see how easy it would be to build up a com-

Fig. 58   Abstract white mohair weave in a wooden frame

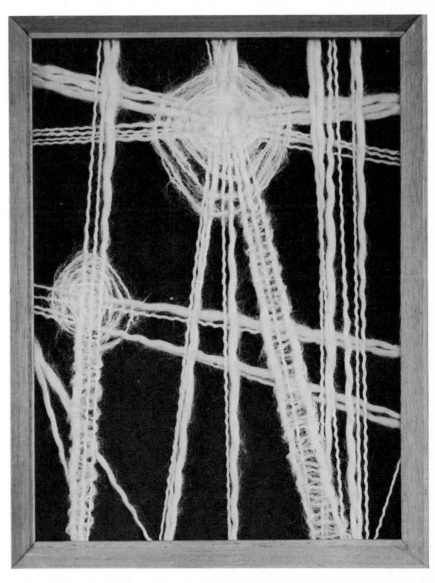

pletely abstract design using this method, which is simply doodling with thread (fig. 58). It is a good idea to produce an unplanned piece of work in this way because one of the pitfalls of weaving is that you over-plan and leave no room for happy accidents. You may find your doodle looks a mess but look again, this time analytically, and you may well see some effects which you could use in another piece of work. No piece of work is ever wasted; you will find that you have always learned something during its construction.

Planning a woven abstract design

Using a new frame, begin thinking a little about what you have learned. Plan where you put your nails, now you know the effects you can obtain. Remember, when using a frame, that nails can be placed at the front and the back of the frame and that threads can be worked across the front nails, above the back nails or above or across a combination of both. In this way you will be able to build up a relief effect. Don't be afraid to experiment with yarns. Combine textured and smooth, thick and thin, and make a note of the results for future reference.

Working a lace-like fabric

While working with home-made square frames, here's an idea you might like to try. With this frame, the work is removed when it is finished so the frame can be used many times. It's a technique that was popular in the 1930s and early 1940s, when it was used to produce place mats. Begin with a small frame, because this technique lends itself to a lot of experimenting. Use a frame about twelve inches by twelve inches and space nails at one-inch intervals around the frame. It is important that the nails on the parallel sides of the frame correspond to one another. Begin with a fluffy yarn like mohair and knot it to a corner nail. Take the yarn, pass it round an adjacent nail and down to pass round its opposite on the parallel side, then bring it round and back up again (fig. 59). This means that a 'U' shape is formed at one end and that each pair of nails holds a looped thread. Continue working across the frame until all the nails have been worked. Now work down the adjacent sides in the same way, until you have formed a grid of mohair threads. Tie the finishing end to the last nail. Now, using a contrasting thread like a lurex knitting yarn, begin at one corner and work across in a diagonal way, putting three loops of yarn on each pair of nails (fig. 60). Work until you reach the opposite corner and tie off your yarn. Finish with a final set of diagonal threads at right angles to the previous set. The next stage is more intricate. Use a needle threaded with lurex, and interweave at each cross-over point to include all the threads, using the method shown in fig. 48. Do just enough weaving to prevent the threads from moving, then fasten off at the back of the work and move on to the next intersection. Continue in this way until all the intersections

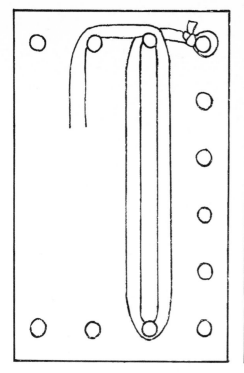

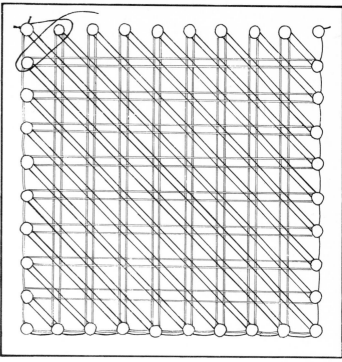

Fig. 59 Hooking the yarn round the nails for the net-like fabric

Fig. 60 Finished appearance of the 'net' fabric

Fig. 61 Working the intersection in the 'net' fabric

have been woven (fig. 61). Using a pair of sharp scissors, cut through all the lurex threads at their mid-way points between the intersections. The resulting fabric should have lurex tassels held by a gossamer mohair net. A large piece of this fabric would make an attractive and individual shawl.

String-and-nail designs

While you are working with nails, why not try a string-and-nail picture? These pictures are usually worked out beforehand in a very mathematical way by planning on graph paper. Normally the nails or panel pins are placed at very regular intervals and the thread is wound around the nail heads to form abstract shapes. At the moment string-and-nail pictures are very popular and there are kits available which produce rather elegant gold and silver shapes on a velvet or wooden background. These kits of course are expensive and mass-produced. It is more rewarding to design your own original pattern.

Materials you will need

A box of panel pins or similar small nails.
A hammer.
A ball of thread (not too stretchy).
A board (something similar to chipboard will do).
A background to cover your chipboard surface; either paint or fabric.
Two sheets of graph paper the same size as your chipboard.
A pencil.
A long ruler.

Planning a graph design

Use one piece of graph paper to sketch out a few rough ideas. For example, try spacing your dots at half-inch intervals around a particular shape. Use one of these dots and join it to all the others with a ruled line. You should have a radiating effect like the rays of the sun. In fig. 62 this radiating effect has been worked around a circle. Now try joining dot to dot across the shape. The design in fig. 63 was worked in this way. By combining these two methods, a satisfactory design will soon emerge. Don't forget to experiment with different yarns too.

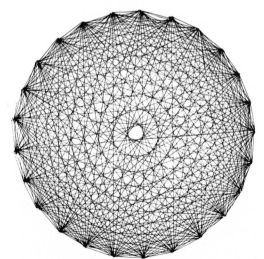

Fig. 62 A string-and-nail design, radiating from one nail to form a circle

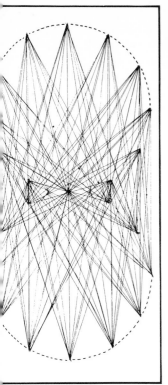

Fig. 63 A string-and-nail design worked across several nails to form an abstract shape

Preparing your baseboard

Once your graph is finished it is time to prepare your chipboard base. This base can be treated in a number of ways, one of which is to cover it with a fabric, like velvet, felt or hessian. Take the fabric round the board and fasten to the back with glue, staples or tacks. The base could also be painted, perhaps in several colours to accentuate the thread-and-nail design. Paper collage or relief work in fabric and glue could be tried or even a repeat of the graph design painted on the base board to create an optical effect. These are some of the possibilities available to you. Don't be content to reproduce the work of others, try to be as original as possible. Perhaps you don't want your thread and nail picture to be too mathematical—in which case try approaching it in a freer way, with nails set more or less at random.

Working from a graph design

If you decide to use your graph design it must be secured to the baseboard, because you will be hammering your panel pins through the graph paper and into the baseboard. Once the nails are in position you can either remove your graph design carefully and work from it as it lies by the side of your baseboard or you can leave it in position and work the threads on top. In this case to remove the graph at the end of the work you will have to tear it, and there is always the possibility that you might break a thread, which would be a catastrophe. It is a good idea to put a touch of glue at each point where a thread and nail meet to prevent any slipping of the thread, but be careful not to drop glue on to the background.

To begin and end work

Knot the thread as inconspicuously as possible around a nail at the beginning and end of the work. Sometimes the addition of glue to the knot means that excess thread can be trimmed off close to the knot.

Shaped frames

The most obvious shaped frame is the circle. One of the easiest shaped frames to weave on is a pair of hoop earrings. Not only are they cheap, they are also rigid and an ideal size for a practice piece.

Working on hoop earrings

First, work a buttonhole covering over the wire hoop (fig. 64), using sewing cotton to prevent any threads that are used later from sliding on the metal surface. Then, still using sewing cotton and working from one side to the other, put down some warp threads in a radiating pattern, passing them

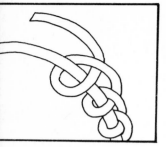

Fig. 64   Buttonholing on a hoop shape

through the buttonholing each time. When the circle is filled to your satisfaction begin thinking about the design for the weft threads. Refer back to the chapters on needleweaving and on circular cards and you may find the beginnings of ideas among your previous experiments.

Once you have completed your hoop earrings try working on a larger scale—for example on an embroidery hoop. When starting, it does help to put the buttonholing around the hoop. Later, as you develop more proficiency in the technique, you will develop your own methods of anchoring threads. You can put a radiating warp on your hoop if you wish, but why not try another idea.

Design ideas for shaped frames

Work a series of threads across your hoop to produce a ribbon of weaving. Work another set of warp threads at right angles to the ribbon, putting some of the threads above the ribbon and some below. When you reach the cross-over point of the two sets of threads you can work a section of kilim weaving and your ribbon will interlock through the work. Try also extending some of your weft threads out to become warps (see colour plate opposite page 40). While working with hoops, make a selection of sizes in wire, link them together, add a necklet and you have a bold and original piece of jewellery (fig. 50).

Up to this point, your weaving has been worked on home-made frames or 'found' frames. There is one frame that is manufactured and can be used over and over again to produce an excellent variety of items from rugs to wall hangings, and that is the rug frame.

The rug frame

The rug frame has been introduced at the end of the chapter because it is much larger than anything you will have worked on before. By this stage, however, you will have produced several pieces of work and so a large frame should not seem too formidable. The rug frame is composed of four sides that slot into one another and are held in position by dowelling pegs. It has two notched dowelling rods for holding the warp threads and two flat bars with wing-nuts to hold the warp threads against the frame (fig. 65).

Setting a warp on a rug frame

To set a warp on the rug frame, measure a length of yarn as long as the frame, double this and allow another four inches. This length is looped in half and tied around one of the notches on the dowling bar. Fill all the notches in this way. Place this round bar as shown in fig. 65, with a flat bar underneath. Do not tighten the wing-nuts at this stage. Make sure all the lengths are straight;

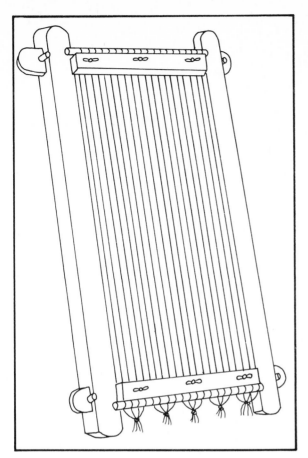

Fig. 65   *A rug frame*

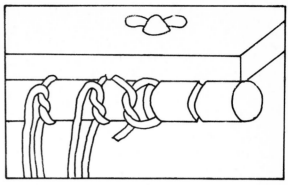

Fig. 66   *Tying the warp around dowelling notches*

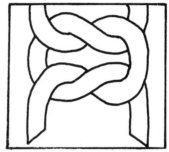

Fig. 67   *The completed knot*

it is most important that they do not cross over one another. Lay your frame flat, and place the second dowelling bar and flat bar in position. Do not tighten the wing-nuts yet. Working from the centre of your threads, match notch to notch and work outwards in each direction. Begin by tying one half of a knot around the notched bar and pull tight (fig. 66). Make sure at all times that your warp threads have not become tangled. When you have completed the tying, tighten the wing-nuts on the first bar. This will cause the knots you have tied to loosen and slide up. Now tighten the wing-nuts on the second bar—once again your half-knot will move. You must now tighten your warp. Working from the centre to the outside try to tension your warp threads as tight as you can. If you place the palm of your hand across the warp threads you will feel if any are slack. When you are satisfied that they are at an equal tension, tie the second half of the knot (fig. 67). Your warp is now completed. Until now, the small items that you have woven have been produced fairly quickly. On the larger rug frame, to pass your weft over and under every warp thread is time consuming and can become tedious. To save time a warp-lifting device is used.

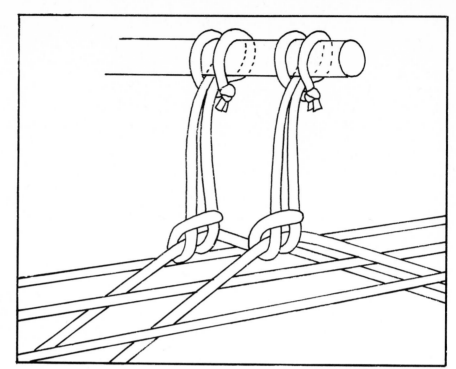

Fig. 68 Fastening string
healds

Fig. 69 Gauge used to
make string healds

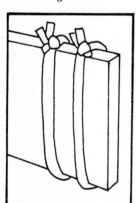

Fig. 70 The shed stick
and harness in use

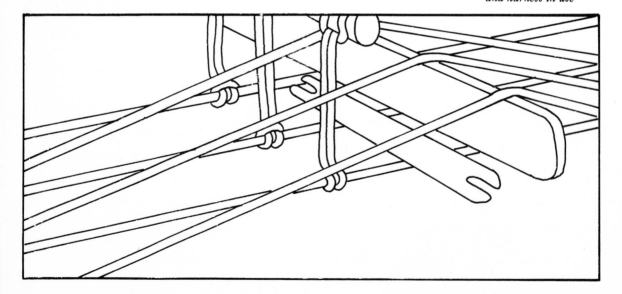

Making a warp-lifting mechanism

In fig. 68 you can see the device in action. On a more sophisticated loom, this lifting device is called a harness or a shaft and each individual string section is a heddle or a heald. The harness raises every alternate warp thread. Each string heald needs to be the same length so it is usual to use a gauge; the width should be about five inches (fig. 69). Make enough healds for every alternate warp thread.

Fitting the heald

Pass the loop of the heald under a warp thread and pass the knot of the heald through this loop, making a slip knot round the warp thread. Continue to do this on each alternate warp thread (fig. 68).

Finishing the harness

Using a piece of dowelling the width of your frame, loop the knotted end of each heald around the dowelling, as shown in fig. 69. You have now completed your harness. This harness will raise one set of warp threads. The second set are raised by using a shed stick (fig. 70).

The shed stick

This is a flat stick the width of the frame, usually rounded off at each end. A long ruler or similar object could be used. This stick is interwoven between the warp threads to pick up those threads not held by the harness; so when you hold the stick in a vertical position it raises one set of threads. To raise the other set, flatten the stick and raise the harness.

The shed

The shed is the space formed between the warp threads when one set are raised. The shuttle is passed through this space.

The stick and harness method explained here is the easiest of lifting mechanisms and will produce a simple plain weave. To produce patterns within the weaving it is necessary to add another harness for each pattern area.

5 Simple looms

You will need to know a few more weaving terms in this chapter. The most important ones you already know, but once you work with a loom it will help if you know all the parts and the variety of equipment connected with it.

The parts of a loom

Even the simplest box loom will have a roller at front and back for carrying the unwoven warp and the woven cloth.

The *warp beam* or *roller* holds the unwoven warp threads at the back of the loom.

The *cloth beam* or *roller* holds the fabric that you have woven at the front of the loom.

The *back beam* supports the warp threads as they pass from the warp beam through the loom.

The *breast beam* supports the woven fabric as it passes through the loom on to the cloth beam.

The *heddle*. The warp threads pass from the back to the front of the loom, through the heddle. The heddle can be rigid, as in a box loom, or composed of a number of harnesses or shafts.

The *harness* or *shaft* holds a series of healds.

The *heald* holds a single warp thread.

The *reed* is a rigid object situated between the breast beam and the heddle. It is composed of a series of stiff wires held in place at top and bottom. With a box loom (fig. 71) the rigid heddle also acts as a reed. There are different sizes of reed and these gauge the weight of the cloth that you produce. Each time you weave a row or pick, the reed

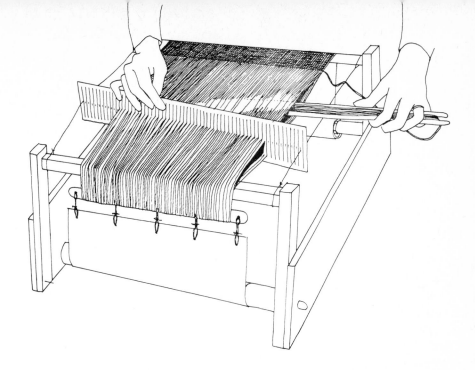

Fig. 71   The box loom

is used to press the weft firmly into the warp threads. The space
between each rigid wire is called a dent. A reed is measured in dents
to the inch. A six reed has six dents or spaces to the inch.

Each dent normally holds a warp thread, sometimes two threads and oc-
casionally none, if you are working on a spaced warp.

Weaving equipment

The *shuttle*. You will have already worked with card shuttles. A loom
shuttle is a longer, wooden version used to carry the weft yarn.

The *shed sticks*. Also sometimes called cross sticks, these are put
through the cross of the warp and used to hold the warp threads in
position for threading up and weaving. The cross will be explained
when warping is described.

The *threading hook* is rather like a fine, flat crochet hook set in a wooden
handle. It is flat to allow for easy insertion through a heald. The func-
tion of the threading hook is to pick up a single warp thread and pull
it through a heald.

The *reed hook* is an elongated S-shaped piece of metal. It is made to fit
into an individual dent in a reed. Its purpose to pull the warp thread
or threads through the reed.

The *raddle* appears superficially like a clumsy reed (fig. 72). It is used to
space the warp threads to the correct width while they are being
wound on to the warp beam. The spaces between the raddle pegs
measure half an inch. A home-made raddle can be made by
hammering nails at half-inch intervals into a length of wood.

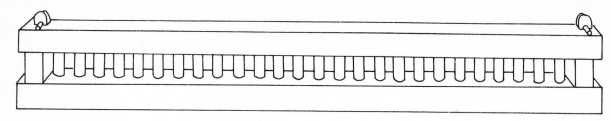

Fig. 72 The raddle

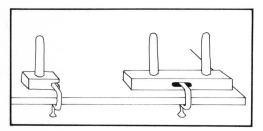

Fig. 74 Warping posts

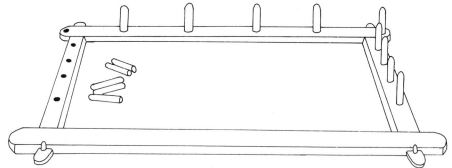

Fig. 73 The warping
frame

Warping frame or *warping posts*. A warping frame (fig. 73) is used to
make a warp up to ten yards in length. It is a four-sided frame in
which are bored a series of holes. These holes are fitted with
adjustable pegs in different positions, depending on the length of
warp required. Warping posts (fig. 74) are clamped to a table edge
and can be used to make smaller warps.

The *spool-holder*. As the name suggests, the spool-holder holds the reels
or spools of yarn when the warp is being made. It is not an essential
item, as spools can be placed in a jar or bowl on the floor during
warping.

Looms

There are four simple looms and these are the only ones which will be discussed in this chapter.

The box loom

The box loom is the simplest of the four looms. It is, as the name suggests, a
box shape and possesses a rigid heddle. The rigid heddle has a dual purpose:

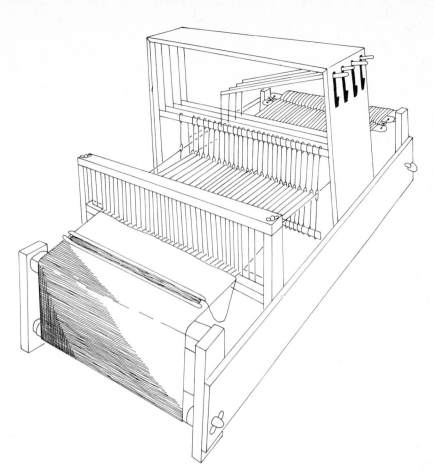

Fig. 75   A table loom

it is used as a heddle and a reed. The heddle is set at thirteen warp threads to the inch. This loom produces only plain weave but, as has already been demonstrated in previous chapters, a plain weave provides no limitations to creative design ideas.

The two-harness table loom

This loom will weave wider widths than the box loom and it has a slotting mechanism for holding the harnesses in position when weaving. The reed size can be varied to cope with different weights of yarn. This loom produces only plain weave (fig. 75).

The four-harness table loom

This loom is obtainable in larger sizes and will weave to forty-five inches in width. The loom will weave not only plain and twill weaves but a variety of other patterns. It has a slot mechanism to hold each harness individually, allowing the weaver to work with speed and precision (Fig. 75).

The vertical rug loom

This loom, unlike the three other looms, rests on the floor and is operated by pedals. It possesses two harnesses which are operated by two pedals. The reed lies horizontally and is prevented from falling by the use of springs set at either side; otherwise the layout of the loom is similar to a horizontal loom. This loom is most suitable for tapestry-type rugs and has the added advantage that work can be viewed in a vertical position while it is being woven.

Making a warp
Choosing a yarn

Any yarn that is used for a warp must be fairly strong. Some hairy yarns will rub and tangle if used in a warp. Some have bits of wool spun loosely into them and these can rub off during the friction of weaving and cause threads to break. To begin with choose a smooth, well-spun yarn that is not too stretchy. If you are in any doubt about using a yarn try the rub test between your thumb nail and forefinger; if the yarn breaks it will not stand up to wear on a loom. When planning your warp, do not mix a very stretchy yarn, like some wools, with a less stretchy yarn like cotton, because you may experience difficulty in obtaining an even tension on your warp threads.

Designing your warp

Your main problem is to decide what exactly you are going to produce on your warp. Is it going to be a fabric for a garment, a furnishing, a tapestry or a rug? Something of a middle weight would be a sensible starting point. Work with cotton as this will not break so easily as a wool yarn. Pick yourself a medium cotton yarn, similar in appearance to a crochet or knitting cotton, in two or three colours. You now have to pick a suitable reed.

Choosing the correct reed

Pick a reed with fine dents and try one thread of your yarn in a dent. Pull your yarn backwards and forwards through the reed; if it rubs or sticks, then you need a coarser reed. If the reed seems too coarse for your yarn, try two threads in a dent. Make sure that both threads can pass one another within the dent; if they don't, your dent is too narrow and you will need a coarser reed. Remember you can have one or two warp threads through a dent. The main criteria is whether there is any friction on the warp threads as they pass through the dent. Once you have chosen your reed, you will be able to calculate how many warp ends to the inch.

Calculating how many warp ends to the inch

Suppose for example, you have decided to use a ten reed with two threads through each dent. A ten reed means there are ten spaces to the inch. As you have two threads through each space, you will have twenty warp threads or ends to the inch. This would be written down as twenty e.p.i. (ends per inch). *To calculate a sample warp.* Let's assume for simplicity that your warp is in one colour. You want your sample to be six inches wide, and a reasonable length to allow for several experiments, say two yards. Allow another eighteen inches for wastage in a table loom and twenty-four inches in a rug loom. The calculation will look as follows:

> 20 ends (warp threads) per inch × 6 (six inches is the width of the sample = 120 ends in the warp
> 2½ yards (length of the warp) × 120 = 300 yards (number of yards of yarn required to make warp).

It is possible to calculate how many yards you have in a hank of yarn by weighing it. Each type of yarn has a different number of yards per hank, also depending on the count of your yarn. To refresh your memory, yarns are supplied in different thicknesses and different plies. For example 2/20s is a two-ply yarn made up of two threads of twenty-thickness wound together. If we use this 2/20s as an example throughout, the calculation should be easier. Cotton has 840 yards per hank. Calculate how many yards for a 2/20 yarn as follows. Divide the ply into the thickness, thus:

> 2/20 = 10
> 840 × 10 = 8400 yards per pound.
> Linen has 300 yards per hank: 300 × 10 = 3000 yards per pound.
> Yorkshire wool has 256 yards per hank: 256 × 10 = 2560 yards per pound.

Now, to give one more example, your yarn this time is 4/4s. Divide ply into thickness 4/4 = 1 thus:

> Worsted wool has 560 yards per hank: 560 × 1 = 560 yards per pound.

Each type of yarn has a different number of yards per pound. I have given you the four most used ones. There are several different types of wool each with different yards per pound, but this will only confuse you at this stage.

Your warping frame is usually one yard long. To make a two and a half yard warp, twice this length will have to be used so the warp doubles back on itself (fig. 76). There are two methods of warping. The simplest is also the slowest. You will need to master the faster method eventually if you wish to produce wide warps.

Warping—simple method

Refer to fig. 76 during this explanation otherwise you may become confused. Warping is a method of measuring off the correct length of yarn for your warp.

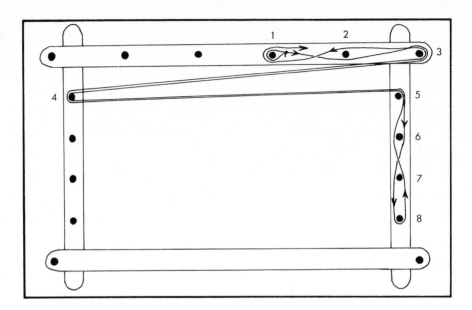

Fig. 76 Warping on a frame

1. Put your spool in a bowl and tie the free end of yarn loosely to peg 1.
2. I usually warp with the board leaning against a wall but to begin it is easier to lay the frame in a horizontal position. Pass your yarn under peg 2 and around peg 3.
3. Cross the frame to peg 4 and pass around this peg.
4. Work back across the frame to pass round peg 5. You have now measured off over two yards of yarn.
5. Passing down the outside of the frame to peg 6.
6. From the outside of peg 6 pass to the inside of peg 7 and down and around peg 8.
7. From the outside of peg 8 work to peg 7, then across to the inside of peg 6, and back to the outside of the frame to pass round peg 5.
8. Work across to peg 4 and then 3, following the previous path.
9. From the outside of peg 3 take the yarn to the outside of peg 2 then across to the inside of peg 1 and around, ready to start on the journey again.

At this stage a pause is necessary to explain the necessity of crossing the threads between 1 and 2 and 6 and 7.

The cross

The cross between pegs 1 and 2 keeps each thread separate from its neighbour. The warp threads may overlap each one, within reason, anywhere between pegs 2 to 5 but you must not lose the continuity of the cross. Not until you have attempted threading the loom will you realize the importance of the cross.

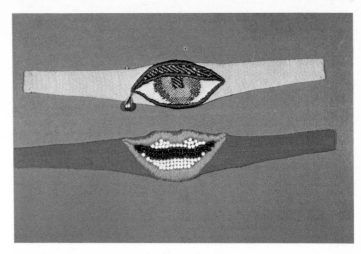

Above: *Two woven chokers.*

Left: *A pastel grey, yellow, pink and blue Rya rug.*

Below (Left): *Suede, fur, leather and wool used in a black wool warp.*

(Right): *Abstract tapestry in white, brown and black.*

*A weaving on an old bicycle wheel. The design is based on
a stained-glass window.*

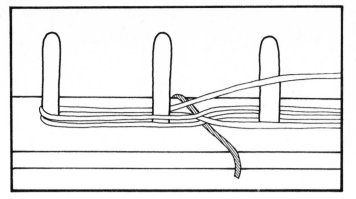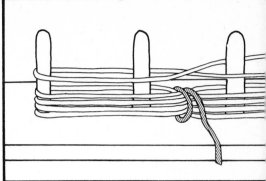

Counting the warp threads

The counting of the warp threads takes place between pegs 6 and 7. Take a contrasting thread measuring just over twice the width of your proposed warp. For example, if your width is six inches the thread will be approximately fourteen inches. This contrasting thread is placed across the frame between pegs 6 and 7 (fig. 77). As you continue making your warp, the threads will lie one on top of the other. When you have laid down ten threads this will be equal to half an inch in our example warp. Bring your contrasting thread over these ten threads from each side and enclose them (fig. 78). In the diagram only eight threads are shown. At every ten threads bring the contrasting thread across again. When you have worked twelve bunches you will have completed six inches. You normally measure every half inch because that is the space in the raddle. If your raddle had one-inch spaces you would measure in inches instead. If you wish to work half-inch stripes in your warp, break off one colour after ten threads have been laid down and join in the second colour by knotting to the previous colour. This joining knot should be positioned at either peg 1 or peg 8 as these mark each end of your warp. Continue working stages 1 to 9 until you have worked six inches of warp. Fasten off in the same way as you started with a tied loop.

Tying the warp

1. Using lengths of contrasting thread, loop an eight-inch length through the warp at peg 8, making sure all the threads are included.
2. Tie a similar length through the warp at peg 1 making sure you include the beginning and ending loops.
3. Knot the ends of the half-inch marker thread firmly together. Leave this tie with plenty of slack thread.
4. Using a fourteen-inch length pass this down one side of the cross at pegs 1 and 2, underneath and up the other side. This length must include all the threads and must pass in the spaces between the pegs

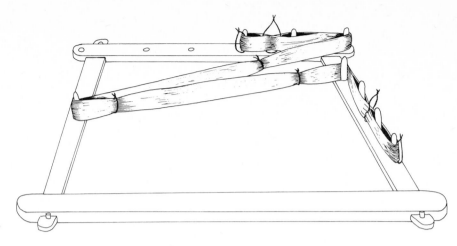

Fig. 79　*Tying up the warp*

and the cross. If in doubt, consult fig. 79. Knot the ends together leaving some slack in the length.

5. The final three ties are between pegs 3, 4 and 5. These ties can be tied quite tightly.
6. To remove the warp from the frame, loosen and remove peg 1, 3, 4, 5 or 8 and the warp will slacken.

Collecting in the warp

To remove the warp always begin at peg 1. The normal procedure is to chain the warp. To do this, pass your hand through the loop formed in the warp around peg 1. Grasp the body of the warp and pull it through the looped section. Insert your hand through this section and repeat the process. With a small warp, like this sample, it is probably easier to wind it neatly between the palm of your hand and your elbow. Always make sure that the end with the counted inches protrudes several inches from the chain or skein to prevent tangling.

Warping—complex method

This method enables you to work a number of warp threads at the same time. Where with the simple method you laid down a thread at a time, with the complex you can wind ten or more threads together. To use this method, however, you really need a spool holder and a separate spool for each thread that you lay down. In fig. 80 the spool holder contains six spools. If you were working a design with twelve ends to the inch, this would mean that you laid down half an inch with one circuit of the warping frame, thus the method is a great time saver. To work stripes, you merely break off one set of colours and join in another, just as you do with the simple method. The major difficulty with this technique is to master the production of the cross between pegs 1 and 2. Refer to fig. 80 for help.

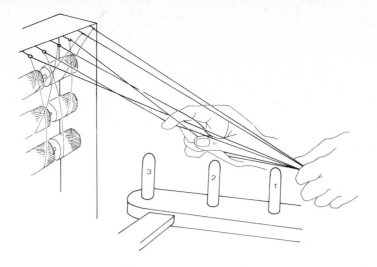

Fig. 80 *Warping using the complex method*

Working the cross—complex method

1. Gather up the six ends from your spools, knot them firmly together and hold them in your left hand.
2. Pull the ends out about eighteen inches and hold them taut.
3. Turn to face these threads which should cross in front of you in a radiating way.
4. With your right hand held with the thumb and forefinger extended and the rest of the hand clenched, begin as follows.
5. Place your thumb firmly on the lowest thread, then as though you were climbing a thread, ladder with your thumb and forefinger, push your forefinger up under the same thread and pass it around and down on the thread above. You should have worked a figure of eight if you have worked the movement correctly. Keeping to the figure of eight, bring your thumb around and down on the thread above, making sure your forefinger lies underneath this thread. Continue working this ladder-like motion until all the threads are collected, forming a cross between your thumb and forefinger.
7. Transfer the cross to your warping board between pegs 1 and 2 (fig. 81).
8. Make sure the beginning knot is correctly positioned on the outside of peg 1.
9. Gather up all the slackness in the warp threads, then continue warping as you did for the simple method.
10. Remember your counting cross will still need to be marked with a contrasting thread, but you don't have to work a cross with the thumb and forefinger as you did between pegs 1 and 2. On the return journey don't forget to work another finger cross between pegs 1 and 2, then pass the whole warp around peg 1 and you are ready to start again. Continue working the warp in this way. To remove the warp, follow the instructions given for the simple method.

Simple looms 59

Putting the warp on the loom

Equipment you will need:

> A raddle.
> Some lengths of twine—to fasten the raddle to the loom.
> A selection of flat sticks the length of which is the same as the width of the roller. (Newsprint can be used in place of the flat sticks.)
> Two cross sticks (see fig. 85).
> Two long sticks, the length of the loom.

Take up your raddle. If it is not a home made one it will have a removable top. Take the top off the raddle and tie the base firmly on to the flat upper surface of the back beam. The raddle must be immovable in this position.

Remove the reed from its holder (called the beater), likewise with a rigid heddle. If the loom has individual healds, divide the numbers of healds centrally and slide them towards each side of the loom. You need to clear the centre area of your loom.

At the back and front of the loom, attached to the cloth and warp beams, is a canvas apron. The canvas apron should have eyelets inserted in it and through these pass lengths of twine that hold a single flat stick in position. This flat stick is passed through the loop formed in your warp where peg 8 was inserted. To fasten the warp on to the warp beam, calculate roughly the centre of your beam. Remember your sample is six inches wide, so you need to situate your warp in a central area six inches wide. Slide the flat or apron stick out of the twine loops but only as far as is necessary to insert the stick through your warp. Spread your warp by removing the contrasting tie placed in one end. Don't try and cram the warp in between the twine loops of one area of the apron stick, allow it to spread to a full six inches (fig. 82). If you find it necessary to retie a twine loop, the method used is shown in fig. 83.

Putting the warp through the raddle. Mark the central six-inch area on your raddle. Gather up your warp, bring it to the outside of the loom and position it to pass over your raddle. Using the half inches in your counting cross, slide each half-inch bunch into one space in your raddle.

Raddling. Take the chained part of your warp and place it through the central clear area of your loom. The reasons for raddling are as follows:

1. To obtain a six-inch width of warp threads throughout the whole warp.
2. To give an even tension to your warp threads.
3. To wind the warp on to the warp beam.
4. To straighten out any tangled threads.

When your warp is positioned in the raddle, place the top on the raddle. Position yourself at the side of the loom with one hand grasping the warp through

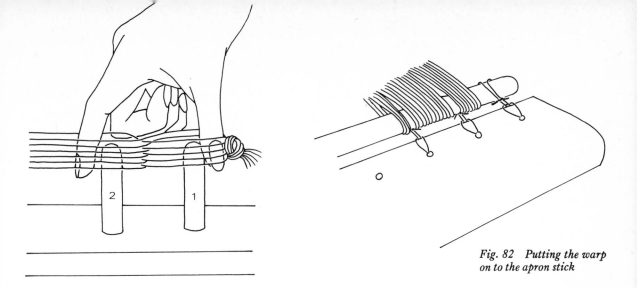

Fig. 82 Putting the warp
on to the apron stick

Fig. 81 Transferring the
cross to the warping frame

Fig. 83 Tying the twine
loop on to the apron

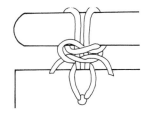

the loom (fig. 84) and the other hand ready to wind the warp beam. Keep an even tension on all the warp threads by allowing your fingers to claw through the warp rather than merely grasping it. During the winding, insert sheets of newsprint or flat sticks into the warp as it is wound on to the warp beam. These sticks should lie between each layer of warp threads to keep the tension even. As you reach a tie in the warp, remove it, give the warp a shake, and re-exert tension. *Do not* remove the cross tie or the end tie. Continue winding until you have reached the cross. With wider warps two operators are needed, one to wind the warp and one to exert tension.

Inserting the cross sticks. The cross on your warp will probably be situated about six inches from the end of your warp. Ideally, the cross needs to be pushed back until about eighteen inches of space is left between warp end and the cross. Do this carefully by working across the warp section by section, rather than attempting the whole warp at the same time. Leave the cross tie in position at all times. The sticks that are used to mark the cross are usually flat with rounded ends and each one has a hole bored in each end (fig. 85). Using a length of twine, knot the two sticks together leaving a two-inch gap between them. Insert the sticks following exactly the path of the cross tie thread. Double check that your sticks are correctly positioned, then tie the remaining ends of the stick together. Remove the tie.

Positioning the cross sticks.

1. Face the front of the loom, that is the end where the reed is positioned.
2. Slide the two long sticks (the length of the loom) through the loom, one at each side. These rest on the back and the breast beams.
3. Place the cross sticks on these two long sticks and position them to lie just behind the harnesses or, in the case of a box loom, in the back part of the box.

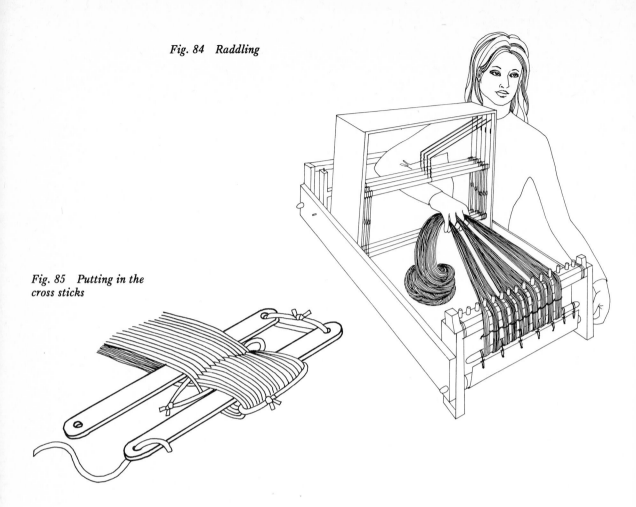

Fig. 84   Raddling

Fig. 85   Putting in the cross sticks

Threading up

Equipment required:

> Threading hook.
> Reed hook.
> Scissors.
> Some contrasting thread.

You have already calculated how many threads there are in your warp. You now have to work out how many threads you will put on each harness, if you have more than one, or where to start if you are using a rigid heddle. Gather up your warp end, cut through the end loop and remove the tie. Use a twenty-four inch length of contrasting thread folded in half. Loop this around your warp end in a self-tightening loop, then tie the remaining ends to the breast beam. On some looms you will need a length longer than twenty-four inches to accomplish this.

Threading up using a rigid heddle

Count up the number of spaces and holes that you have in your heddle. From this amount subtract the number of threads in your warp. The number left represents the number of holes and spaces that will not be filled with warp threads. These spaces should be placed equally at either end of the heddle. When you have calculated the number of spaces to be left empty, place a contrasting thread through the heddle to mark the place at each end.

Use of the cross sticks. If you look at your cross sticks, you will see how the warp threads emerge one under a stick, one over a stick. Each one has its place and if you try and pick up one out of turn it will pull on adjacent threads. Beginning at one end of the sticks, pull the first warp thread carefully from the gathered bunch at the front of the loom. Put your threading hook through the first space and pick up the first warp thread. Continue in this way, threading alternate slits and holes. *Make sure* that your threads remain threaded through the cross sticks. As you complete a section of about twenty warp threads, knot the bundle together loosely. This prevents any chance of un-threading. Continue until all the warp is threaded through the rigid heddle. Refer to the paragraph headed 'tying the warp to the cloth beam' (p. 65), to complete the procedure (fig. 86).

Threading up on a two- or four-harness table loom
Calculating the correct number of healds. For a two-harness loom, take the number of warp threads and divide by two. This will give you the number of healds required on each harness.

For a four-harness loom, take the number of warp threads and divide by four.

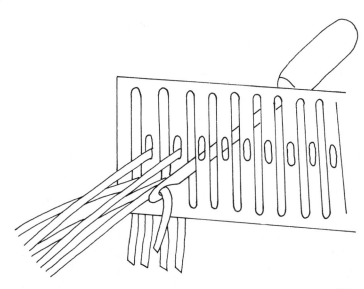

Fig. 86   Threading the rigid heddle

Untie your warp from the breast beam for a moment. Begin with the harness nearest to you and work from the centre. Count out the required number of healds. Any surplus should be divided equally at each end of the harness to maintain the correct balance on the harness. Repeat the process on each harness. Retie your warp to the breast beam and position it so that it lies between the counted healds and any surplus ones; this will keep the two sets apart. You can tie your warp to either side of the loom, but when you begin threading you work from the opposite side to where the warp is tied, therefore if you are right-handed it is easier to begin threading from the right side.

Threading up on a two-harness loom

Count out the required number of healds as already described, then, to work a straight thread-up, continue as follows, referring to the paragraph 'use of cross-sticks' (p. 63).

Take the first warp thread in the cross and loosen it from the tied bundle. *Do not* remove the thread from the cross. Pass your threading hook through the first heald on the nearest harness, called harness 1, pull the thread through. Take up the second warp thread, pass your threading hook through the first heald on the farthest harness, called harness 2, pull the thread through. The third thread pulls through the second heald on harness 1, and the fourth thread pulls through heald 2 on harness 2. Continue zigzagging in this way. When you have threaded about twenty warp threads, loop them together in a loose slip knot. Continue threading up in this fashion.

Threading up on a four-harness loom

Refer to 'use of cross sticks'. Then, for a straight thread-up, work as follows (fig. 87). Take the first thread in the cross and loosen it from the tied bundle. Pass your threading hook through the first heald on the nearest harness, called harness 1, pull the thread through. Take up the second warp thread, pass your threading hook through the first heald on the next harness, called number 2, and pull the thread through. Warp thread 3 passes through the first heald on harness 3 and likewise with warp thread 4 and harness 4. Warp thread 5 passes through heald 2 on harness 1; warp 6 through heald 2 on harness 2 and so on. Threading up is continued in this way. As you work across your warp, loop every twenty threads into a loose slip-knot. This will prevent any accidental unthreading taking place.

Threading the reed. Replace the reed into the beater. Tie the beater in a vertical position (on a horizontal loom). Some looms have holes drilled in the beater and the frame of the loom, where a peg can be inserted to hold the beater in the correct position. Slacken the ratchet on the warp beam to allow

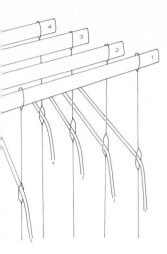

Fig. 87 *Threading a four-harness loom*

more warp to be pulled forward. Allow enough warp to wind forward so that it can reach the breast beam. Find the central six inches of the reed in the same way as when working with a rigid heddle. Don't forget, if you decided to have two threads in a dent, this must be included in your calculations. Working from either end, take up the first warp thread, check that it is correct from the cross and the harness, insert your reed hook through the reed and pull the thread through. At this stage it is easy to allow threads to cross; make sure that yours do not. Tie sets of threads together at one-inch intervals as before, to prevent any chance of them becoming unthreaded.

Tying the warp to the cloth beam. Loosen the cloth beam until the canvas apron lies on the breast beam. Make sure the apron passes on the outside of the beam. Adjust your warp to overlap the apron by four to five inches. Your sections of warp should be divided into groups of about one inch. Take the first group, pass it over the apron stick to divide into two, each length passing under the stick to lie at either side of the warp section (fig. 88). Knot these lengths together in a single knot over the warp section. Repeat this process across the warp.

Tensioning the warp. Each knot must now be pulled tight and adjusted until the tension is the same on all the threads. Start at the middle and work out in each direction. Do this tightening several times and eventually you will obtain an even tension. Test the tension by placing the palm of your hand across the warp threads. You will feel if there is any variation in tension. When you are satisfied, complete the knot as shown in fig. 88.

Fig. 88 *Tying the warp to the cloth beam and the finished knot*

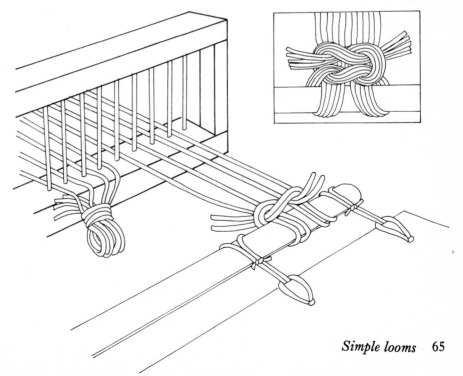

To begin weaving

Rigid heddle

To obtain a shed, that is the space through which the shuttle passes, push down on your warp with the heddle and insert a thin flat stick. To work the second shed required for plain weaving, pull the heddle away from the warp and insert a second flat stick. By inserting sticks in this way you obtain an evenness in your warp threads which makes weaving easier to start. (To remind yourself of how to start weaving refer to figs 41, 43 and 45.)

Two-harness loom

To obtain a shed, push or pull down the control handle for harness 1 and slot into position. Insert a flat stick. To work the second shed, release harness 1 and slot in harness 2. Insert a second flat stick. These movements will work a plain weave. Refer to the section on the rigid heddle for further details.

Four-harness loom

To obtain a shed, pull or push down the control handles for harnesses 1 and 3 simultaneously and slot into position. Insert a flat stick. To work the second shed required for plain weaving, release harnesses 1 and 3 and slot in harnesses 2 and 4 simultaneously. Insert a second flat stick. (Refer to the section on the rigid heddle for details.) With the four-harness loom you can also work a variety of patterns. One you have already experienced is the twill.

To work a simple twill

To obtain a simple 2/2 twill, work the harnesses as follows:

> *First pick:* lift harnesses 1 and 2.
> *Second pick:* lift harnesses 2 and 3.
> *Third pick:* lift harnesses 3 and 4.
> *Fourth pick:* lift harnesses 4 and 1.

Repeat these four picks and you will obtain a twill weave.

Some helpful hints

Making an arc

Making an arc has already been demonstrated in fig. 45. It is a method of ensuring that your selvedges do not begin to creep inwards because you are weaving too tightly.

Weaving rhythm

On a loom you will begin to develop a rhythm to your weaving and it is something like this:

1. Make a shed, beat up once with the reed.
2. Pass through the shuttle, double beat up with the reed.
3. Change shed, beat up once with the reed.
4. Pass through the shuttle, double beat up with the reed.

Each cloth requires a different beat up and it depends on how firmly you apply the reed. You should aim to get the same number of weft threads per inch as there are warp threads to the inch. Sometimes you will beat up less weft than warp, but usually you will find the reverse happens and because of vigorous beating there are too many weft threads per inch. Don't despair, instead don't beat up quite so strongly.

Selvedges

On any large piece of weaving it is usual to put doubled warp threads at each selvedge edge. The selvedges undergo a good deal of friction from the reed and doubled threads reduce the chances of breakages.

Winding on your warp

After you have been working on a piece of weaving for a while you will find it necessary to wind on your warp.

1. Slacken off all your harnesses.
2. Slacken off the warp beam and wind off some warp.
3. Wind on the cloth beam and tighten to the correct tension.
4. Check that your cross sticks are in position near the beam and have not pushed up behind the last harness.

Repairing loose and broken threads.

To repair a broken thread:

1. Break off a fresh length of thread the length of your loom.
2. Trace the breakage, which is usually at the heald.
3. Thread your new thread through the heald and trace it back to the cross sticks.
4. *Do not* break off the old thread. Merely tie it to the new thread using a bow or a similar release knot.
5. Bring the new thread through the reed.
6. Using a dress-maker's pin, pin into the actual cloth about one inch below and parallel to the last weft pick.

7. Wind the new thread in a figure of eight around the pin. Continue weaving until the broken thread is long enough to be rejoined to the weaving, using the pin method already described.

Slackness in the warp threads

Use a pin (in a similar manner to mending broken threads) to take up slackness in a warp thread. All loose threads can be woven into the fabric after it has been removed from the loom.

Always slacken off your warp if you have to leave it for any length of time. This will retain the elasticity of your warp threads.

Some ideas for different warps

Spaced warps

These are basically warps with areas left free of warp threads. When threading up you would not leave healds unthreaded within the harness because they might cause threads to tangle, but when the warp is passed through the reed spaces could be left. In fact, when you have worked a few sample ideas on your first warp, why not redent it with one inch of warp and half an inch of space across its width. As you weave you could try spacing your weft also to see what effects you could obtain.

Tie and dye warps

If you remember, in chapter 2 we discussed dyeing yarn and tie/dyeing by accident. Rather attractive effects can be obtained by tie/dyeing a warp, and the method is quite simple. Make your warp in the usual way, but when it comes to tying the central areas of the warp, plan where you are going to insert your pattern ties. It will normally be stripes that occur.

To tie and dye a two-colour warp

1. Make a warp of yellow yarn.
2. Following the instructions on the dye packet, mix up a red dye-bath.
3. Use either raffia, waxed thread, elastic bands or string for tying. Wind a series of bands, about one inch wide, tightly around your warp (fig. 89). Avoid tying in the areas of the cross and the counting cross. The ties create a resist area where the dye cannot penetrate.
4. Dye your warp in the usual way, rinse it and allow it to dry.
5. Carefully cut the tied bands, avoiding any warp threads, and remove the ties.
6. The resulting warp should be red with yellow stripes.

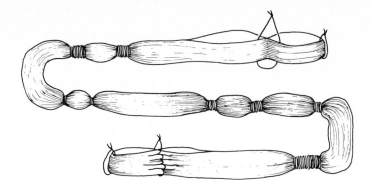

Fig. 89   Tying bands for tie/dyeing

To tie and dye a three-colour warp.

1. Mix up two dye-baths, one in yellow and one in light blue.
2. Make a white warp.
3. Use the yellow dye first. Tie some large areas in the warp.
4. Dye your warp yellow, rinse, and allow to dry until damp and then remove the ties.
5. Retie, leaving undyed white areas free and tieing in yellow areas only.
6. Using the light blue dye, redye the warp.
7. Rinse, dry and remove the ties.
8. The resulting warp should be yellow where the last ties were made, blue where white areas were, and green where the blue dye has mixed with the yellow.

These tie-and-dye methods may have sparked off colour ideas of your own—if not, refer to chapter 1 for examples of colour mixtures!

Dip-dyeing a warp

Ideally, for this method of dyeing, you should have two or three different dyes, mixed up and ready to use at the same time. The method is as follows:

1. Make a white warp and dampen it really well.
2. Using the first dye, for example violet, carefully allow a section of the warp to hang in the dye-bath. If you are using a gas flame to heat the dye bath, be careful you do not scorch your yarn.
3. Rinse the dye completely out of the yarn.
4. Using dye number two, for example turquoise, select an adjacent section and allow the warp to hang in the dye-bath. You will notice that the dye travels up the damp yarn slightly. Use can be made of this effect if desired by allowing the two colours to merge and produce a third colour.
5. Again rinse the dye out of the warp yarn.
6. Repeat the process with a third dye which could be cerise. By allowing an intermingling of the dye colours many beautiful and subtle colour variations can result.

7. You can continue dipping in different colours; or you can try for a rainbow or even a shaded effect, say from pale lemon to yellow, through orange and red to maroon or aubergine.
8. While you are dyeing your warp you could also prepare some hanks of weft yarn and dye them to match your warp.

Stencilled Warps

The stencil is applied to the warp *after* the warp has been put on to the loom. The loom is set up completely as if to begin weaving. The stencil is applied to the back of the warp between the back beam/cross sticks and the rigid heddle/harnesses.

Preparing a stencil

Equipment required:

> Sheet of fine card.
> Sheet of thick card.
> Sharp knife.

Begin by designing a simple geometric pattern, for example a selection of squares, triangles or circles. Your design should lie within the borders of the warp, allowing about half an inch in from each edge.

1. Using the fine card, cut out a square large enough to overlap the edges of the warp, thus protecting them, and include your design area.
2. Using the thick card, cut out a square the same size as the thin card.
3. Transfer your design to the thin card.
4. Cut out your design shapes from the main part of the card, remembering to leave supporting struts (fig. 90). The dye will be applied to the cut-out areas.

Fig. 90   Using a stencil

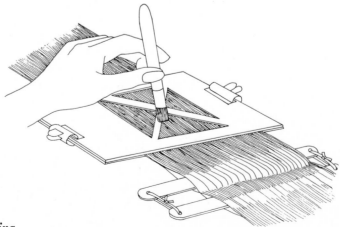

Printing the stencil
Equipment required:

> Stencil.
> Stencil base (that is the thick card square).
> Two bulldog clips.
> Fabric printing ink.
> Stencil brush.
> Waste rag.

1. Place the thick card base under your warp, with the stencil on top. The warp is sandwiched between the two cards.
2. To hold the cards in position, clip each side with a bulldog clip.
3. Put a little fabric printing ink in a mixing dish.
4. Allow the ends of the bristles of your stencil brush to come in contact with the mixture. Test the effect by dabbing firmly on a piece of waste fabric. If the effect is too sticky put less ink on your brush, if powdery put more ink on your brush.
5. When you are satisfied that the consistency is correct, transfer the dye to your warp using the same dabbing motion. Support the warp by placing your other hand underneath the thick card square.
6. Allow the fabric ink to dry before proceeding with your weaving. Several patterns can be applied to your warp in this way. You are not restricted to one colour but it is better to cut a different stencil for each colour and allow colours to dry between applications. The warp can be woven in the normal way.

More tapestry techniques

So far only two simple tapestry techniques have been discussed, those shown in figs 55 and 56—slit (or kilim) and interlocking weaving.

Linking techniques
Dovetailing. Fig. 91 shows the simplest form of dovetailing. Superficially you might think that there is no difference between this technique and the interlocking shown in fig. 56. Interlocking, however, allows the weft threads to interlock with one another; in dovetailing each weft thread passes around a common warp thread. In the simplest form of dovetailing the weft threads alternate with one another. The major disadvantage of this method is that the common warp thread will carry twice as many threads as the other warp threads. This means that if a join by this method is permitted to continue for too long, a hill will begin to form at the junction point.

Fig. 92 shows a decorative dovetail join involving sets of four threads. The method is the same as in the simpler form: each set shares a common warp

Fig. 91   Simple
dovetailing

Fig. 92   Diagram of 4/4
dovetailing

Fig. 93   Brick join in
kilim

thread. Instead of alternating each weft thread, work blocks of four weft threads, alternating the blocks.

Kilim. From fig. 55 you will have worked the simplest form of kilim or slit tapestry. A variation is shown in fig. 93. This diagram demonstrates a brick-like join worked in the kilim technique. The diagram is self-explanatory, showing an overlap of four threads between each brick shape. The number of threads in the overlap can be varied.

Outlining. To accentuate a pattern area, or a join in a design, outlining is sometimes used. To make a vertical outline, the contrasting weft is wound in a figure of eight up two warp threads. The method of making a diagonal is shown in fig. 94. The technique is rather like kilim, but an extra warp thread is left between the pattern areas and the outline thread is wound up the weft by weaving over two threads and back under one. The outline should be worked at the same time as the adjacent woven areas.

Surface techniques

Soumak. Soumak is a method of working a surface rib in a weft direction. It is used in conjunction with plain weaving. Fig. 95 shows the method of encircling each warp thread with the weft. The encircling can be in either direction and if opposite directions are combined in an alternating way, the effect that is obtained is similar in appearance to a knitted fabric. To work the same diagonal on each pick it is necessary to reverse the decorative weft so that the same diagonal is worked on each pick. It is usual to insert one or two picks of

Fig. 94   Outlining in weaving

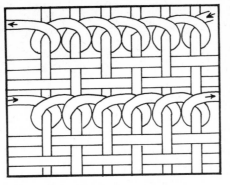

Fig. 95   Soumak

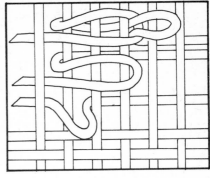

Fig. 96   Working weft chaining

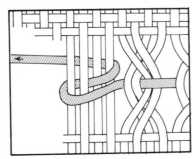

Fig. 97   Leno or gauze weave in detail

plain weave between each decorative row. If you are working with the same yarn for both soumak and plain weave, you can work an extra pick of plain weave and this will return your yarn to the same side of the warp each time, which will make your soumak easier to work.

Weft chaining. Weft chaining will give you a surface effect very similar to two alternate rows of soumak, but on a larger scale (fig. 96). The major advantage of weft chaining is that it is quicker to work than soumak; the disadvantage is that you can only obtain a knitted effect where soumak can give you surface texture with the angles all in the same direction. Weft chaining can be worked over any number of warp threads more than two.

Openwork techniques
The leno or gauze weave. The leno twist is a weaving method which you will have already encountered in the chapter on weaving into and on to fabrics (see fig. 21). It is a method of twisting warp threads around one another and holding them in place with a horizontal weft thread. In fig. 97 the leno twist is sandwiched between two layers of plain weave. There is no reason why several sets of warp threads cannot be interwoven with one another to form an area of lace-like fabric. (Refer also to fig. 22 for a similar openwork technique.)

Imitation filet. In this method both the warp and the weft are spaced out in blocks of two threads. The first pick of weft is a straightforward interweaving between the warp threads, but on the return row the weft passes around the single weft thread plus the paired warp threads, as shown in figs 98 and 99, to form a grid like structure.

Spanish lace. This is a method of weaving on small groups of warp ends and linking them with a continuous weft thread to produce a fancy openwork fabric. Fig. 100 demonstrates the method. Beginning with your first group of warp threads work four picks of weft (it is often easier to work with a small shuttle) and move on to the next set of warp threads. Bring your weft to work in line with the first pick of the previous piece of weaving and work four picks. The weft will curve and form an attractive shape linking the areas of weaving. Fig. 101 shows a similar method of working but linkage is allowed between alternating sets of warp threads.

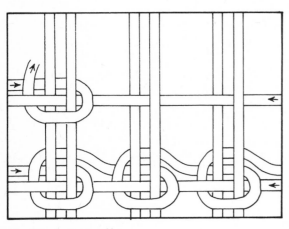

Fig. 98   *Imitation filet*

Fig. 100   *Spanish lace*

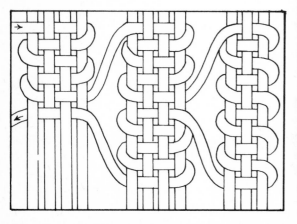

Fig. 99   A completed piece of work showing imitation filet

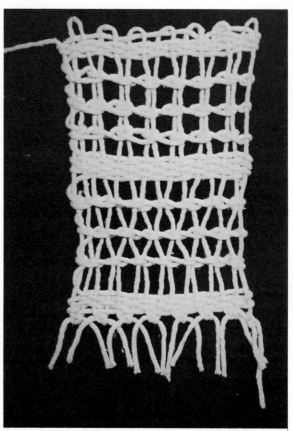

Medallion Weave. This is a method of weaving to produce gathered sections of weft at varying intervals. To introduce this idea into a plain weave area, follow these instructions:

1. Work a pick of heavier contrasting colour.
2. Work four picks in the original yarn.
3. To work the medallion, use the contrast yarn. Put your yarn in the shed only to where the first medallion is to be worked, then pass the shuttle out of the shed to lie on top of the work. Using a crochet hook, loop the contrast yarn over the plain weave pick and under the first contrast pick. Pass your shuttle through the loop and tighten the gathered area. Re-insert the shuttle into the shed and work another medallion in the same way. Fig. 102 shows the medallion worked on a spaced warp, which can be equally effective.

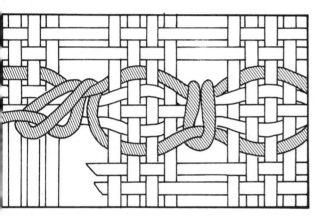

Fig. 102   Working the medallion weave

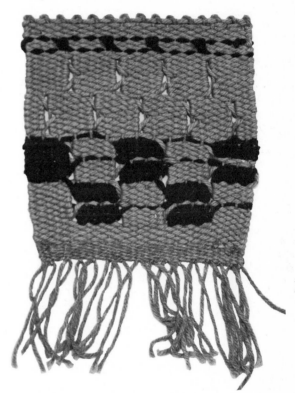

Fig. 101   A variation of Spanish lace

6 Ideas for weaving materials

What shall I use to weave with? The answer is anything and everything. Nearly all the ideas in this chapter were worked on a two-harness loom so most of them, no matter how complex they may look, are based mainly on a plain weave pattern.

Make yourself a long warp of cotton or wool, not too fine and only about six to eight inches wide, because you are going to work out some sample ideas. These samples usually measure about six by eight inches and are test pieces to see what your ideas will look like when they are woven. No matter how experienced you become in weaving, you can never gauge exactly what a piece of weaving will look like, so it is not a bad idea to get into the habit of weaving samples.

Keeping a sample folder

These samples can be kept in a sample folder or sketch-book. When you have finished a sample *always* make a note of the type of yarn you used, your reed size, and your method of threading up. If you are working on a two-harness loom, the thread up is usually the same all the time. That is one warp thread passing through a heald on the front harness, then the next thread passing through a heald on the back harness, and zig-zagging backwards and forwards from harness to harness across the loom. This is a plain thread-up. Should you deviate from this method, perhaps by spacing a warp, then make a note of how this was done. It is surprising how easily you can forget a method; you may at a later date wish to repeat an effect in a larger piece of work and not be able to remember how it was achieved. The purpose of this chapter is to introduce you to just some of the materials you can weave with.

Fabric strips

Using a spaced warp, the first illustration (fig. 103) shows a fine wool weft combined with different thicknesses of cut fabric. It was found that if the cut fabric was too thick it began to wrinkle up. This effect could, of course, be used to produce a piece of ruched material.

Working a fancy leno weave

Using a fine cotton warp and a four-harness loom, the next sample used the leno weaving technique to obtain the spaced effect (fig. 104). The warp is threaded up in blocks. The numbers in fig. 105 represent the harnesses. Try to imagine that you are looking down on the harnesses and that each cross represents a threaded heald. Several adjacent warp threads are threaded alternately on harnesses 1 and 2, rather like a plain weave thread-up on a two-harness loom. The process is repeated on harnesses 3 and 4 as shown. Continue across the warp in this fashion until all the warp threads are threaded.

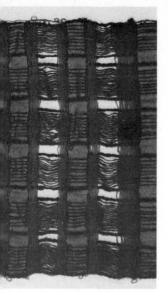

Fig. 103   The spaced warp using cut fabric and wool

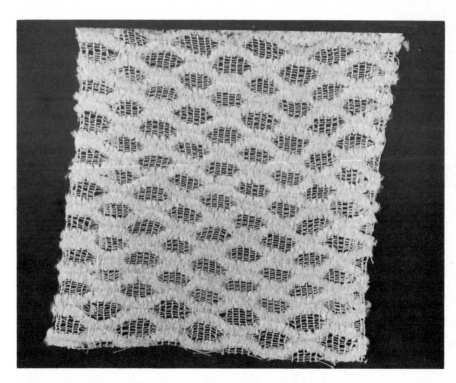

Fig. 104   Chenille/leno weave using fine cotton warp

Fig. 105   The thread-up for the leno example

4									X	X	X	X
3								X	X	X	X	
2		X		X		X		X				
1	X		X		X		X					

Unless you have a loom to try out this technique, you may experience difficulty in visualizing the technique.

First pick. Raise harnesses 1 and 3 and pass through a thick weft. (In the example cotton chenille was used.)

Second pick. Leave harness 3 raised, lower 1 and raise 2. Using a finer yarn (in the example it was a fine cotton), pass your finer weft through, twisting each pair of warp threads in a leno weave. Of course, this applies only to those warps threaded through harnesses 1 and 2.

Third to seventh pick. Leave 3 raised and alternately raise 1 and 2, working a leno weave on each pick using only threads passing through harnesses 1 and 2.

Eighth pick. As first pick.

Ninth pick. Leave harness 1 raised, lower 3 and raise 4. Repeat as for second to seventh picks but this time work your leno weave only on threads passing through harnesses 3 and 4.

Sixteenth pick. As ninth pick.

Making a chenille yarn

While discussing chenille and leno weaves it is worth mentioning that it is possible to make your own chenille yarn on a coarse scale. Make a warp of blocks of three warp threads separated by one-inch spaces. Refer to fig. 106 to see how the leno thread travels across adjacent warp threads. In the diagram only one weft thread is shown. In fact bunches of threads can be passed through on each pick, depending on the fullness of the yarn that you are using. Fig. 107 shows the woven effect. To obtain the final effect cut through your weft threads at the central point between two sets of warp threads and you will be left with a series of pieces of chenille yarn.

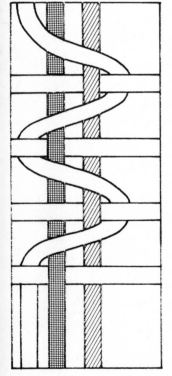

Fig. 106   How the leno thread travels in chenille made on the loom

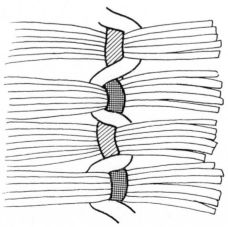

Fig. 107   Chenille yarn when it is woven

Drinking straws and twigs

Before leaving chenille and leno entirely, fig. 108 shows a method of working with blocks of warp threads to produce a heavy leno weave. The weft spacing is in chenille yarn and the fancy effect obtained by using a mohair warp and drinking straws in the weft. By inserting something rigid like drinking straws through a warp, an entirely different concept is given to the weaving: it is no longer pliable in both directions. From working with drinking straws on a spaced warp, I got the idea of using dried flowers and twigs, which can be seen in fig. 109. This idea on a large scale would make an attractive wall hanging and a permanent reminder of the passing of the seasons.

Fig. 108   Drinking straws, chenille and mohair used in a leno weave

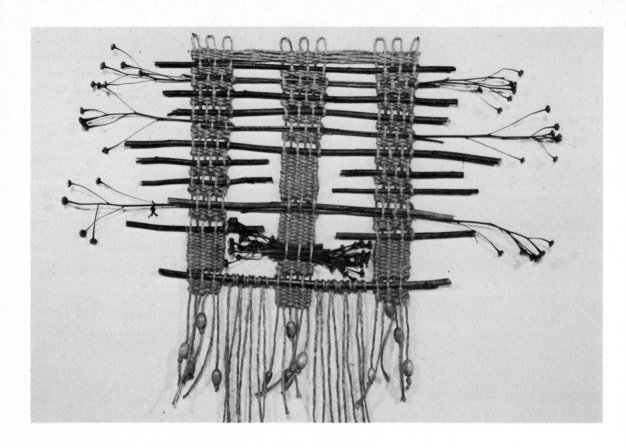

Fig. 109   Twigs and beads used in a jute warp

Parcel string

Parcel string is always interesting to work with, especially the hairy variety. Fig. 110 resulted from dyeing experiments with parcel strings and the discovery of some baling twine. This twine is used to tie up bales of hay. To work a similar sample, dye some parcel string brown and try to obtain some baling twine. The warp was a thick wool, which was also used to start the sample with several plain-weave weft picks. Using undyed parcel twine separated into single unwound pieces, work the outer triangle shapes in soumak with a row of plain weave in between. The dark brown large diamond shape is formed from cut Ghiordes knots (see fig. 128) and the central diamond is uncut Ghiordes knots (see fig. 130) in baling twine. On a large scale this would make a super rug.

Plastic foam sponge

In the process of searching for unusual weft materials I came across foam sponge. A warp and weft sponge weave would make an unusual place mat and could also be used on a large scale to soften a seating area, although it would not stand up to really heavy wear.

Fig. 110 Parcel string and twine used in a wool warp

Reflective materials

In this category you will find some materials that are not commonly used, e.g. matt silver leather in thin strips; sequin cut-outs (the background waste that is left after sequin manufacture) obtainable in long strips usually about three inches wide; and melinex, a mirror-surfaced, metal-coated acetate obtainable in rolls of different thicknesses and widths, was of a similar thickness to the sequin waste and cut initially into strips. It was then shaped to pass over three warp threads and under one. The shaping was made so that a narrow waisted area passed behind a single warp thread, whilst an oval shaped area covered the three warp threads. The result is extremely effective. An idea like this could be used to work an insert in a bodice of an evening dress or an ornate jacket.

Fur and leather

While working with reflective materials I tried working with strips of leather, suede and fur (colour plate opposite page 56). Some of the leather was shaped in a similar way to the melinex but on a smaller scale, and the strips of black fur

Fig. 111 Leather strips and metal chain

Fig. 112 Suede and cur-tain rings

were cut with a knife from the back of a skin. Never use scissors on fur as this cuts the pile. The fur was woven over three warp threads and under one so that it did not become flattened by too many warp threads passing over it. When the sample was finished, a needle was used to pick out any fur trapped behind a warp thread. This method of weaving gives a smooth, sleek appearance to the fur.

Leather used by itself makes some really elegant and relatively inexpensive items. Some of the sample ideas tried are shown here. Fig. 111 shows strips of leather interwoven and fastened to metal chain. Plastic chain, sequins and leather also look good together. In some cases, to prevent too much movement of warp and weft materials, a blob of glue can be used at possible movement points. In fig. 112 a new item was introduced into the interweaving, i.e. curtain rings. The curtains rings not only add a decorative effect but form an important part of the interweaving process. The final fabric is pliable and un-usual and could be used to produce garments.

Small items like belts, necklets, bracelets and armlets are probably the best articles to make in leather because they can be made from small off-cuts. Leather skins are expensive to practise on; it is better to make mistakes on smaller pieces.

Fig. 113   Two chokers, one in black leather, the other in orange suede

Two simple woven necklets

Fig. 113 shows two leather necklets that can be made in about thirty minutes. Take the measurement of your neck; the necklet should be two inches shorter than this measurement. The width is three-quarters of an inch at each end, broadening to one and a half inches at the centre front. In the lower example, vertical slits have been cut into the leather at the centre front. Through these slits thongs of a contrasting colour have been woven. The ends of the thongs have been left long and threaded with a wooden bead at each end. A patch of leather has been stuck behind the woven area to give strength. The end ties are also made of leather thong. Punch a hole in each end of the necklet and pass a thong end through. Make a small slit or hole in the end of the thong and pass the other end of the thong through this slit. Pull the thong tight and it will be firmly fastened to the end of the necklet.

A similar idea is shown in the top necklet, but this time the slits have been cut horizontally in a diamond shape. Contrasting lengths of suede have been woven through and trimmed to a rounded head. The diamond shape is further accentuated by sticking a triangle of suede at each side of the interwoven area.

Making a leather armlet

A reversible armlet can be made along the same lines as the necklets. Once again the length of the armlet is smaller than the circumference of the arm. Slits and interweaving are again used and the ends of the armlet are strengthened with two thicknesses of leather stuck together. These are then punched to allow for a lacing thong.

Ideas for weaving materials   83

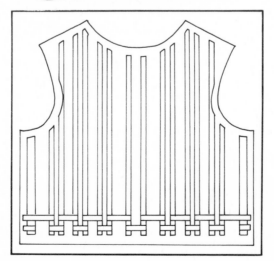

Fig. 114 Man's brown leather jerkin

Fig. 115 The construction of the man's jerkin

Fig. 116   Girl's suede jerkin

Leather slippers

The working of a pair of leather slippers was mentioned on page 36; the grid pattern and method of interlacing the strips are shown in figs 52 and 53.

A leather jerkin

A leather jerkin or jacket is not too difficult to make (fig. 114). Begin with a simple pattern shape, just a plain back and two fronts, with no darts in the pattern. Buy one or two leather skins—enough to fit your pattern. Lay the leather with the wrong side facing you and place your pattern pieces on the leather. Draw around the pieces with a ball-point pen and then remove your pattern. The idea of garment weaving in leather is to waste as little leather as possible. So rather than cutting slits as in fig. 113, aim for the effect shown in fig. 111, that is for spaced-out strips of leather. To do this, first draw a half-

Ideas for weaving materials   85

inch border around your whole pattern. This border must not be cut into at all. Draw a series of vertical lines beginning and ending at the borders. Slit down each of these lines with a knife. Following the line of the border remove each alternate strip of leather (fig 115). The strips that you have removed are now used for the weft and interwoven between the warp strips that are left. Space your weft strips in a similar way to the warp. Glue the intersections where necessary. In the sample shown chain and curtain rings have been added as decoration. Treat both fronts and the back in the same way, then join the jacket at the side and shoulder seams by overlapping. To neaten all the edges and seams back-stitch a strip down each seam and add a shaped strip around the neck and arm-hole edges. The woman's jerkin (fig. 116) is worked in a similar way but areas of plain suede are interspersed with the interwoven panels.

Now that we have explored a few ideas for unusual wefts, let's look at experimental warp materials.

Transparent materials

A transparent plastic warp was used to produce the examples shown in fig. 117. The yarns used are either the transparent plastic itself, or a chenille yarn. Other materials used include fine velvet ribbon (looped or flat) and sequins. I also tried using perspex slats interspersed with polythene strips (fig. 118). This small sample was sufficient to show how effective the idea could be in creating a window blind or window hanging.

Fig. 117   Five samples worked on a transparent warp

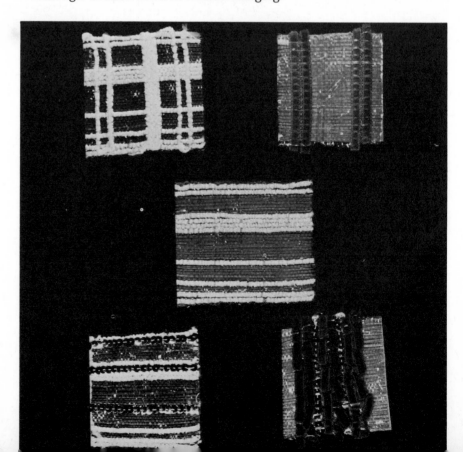

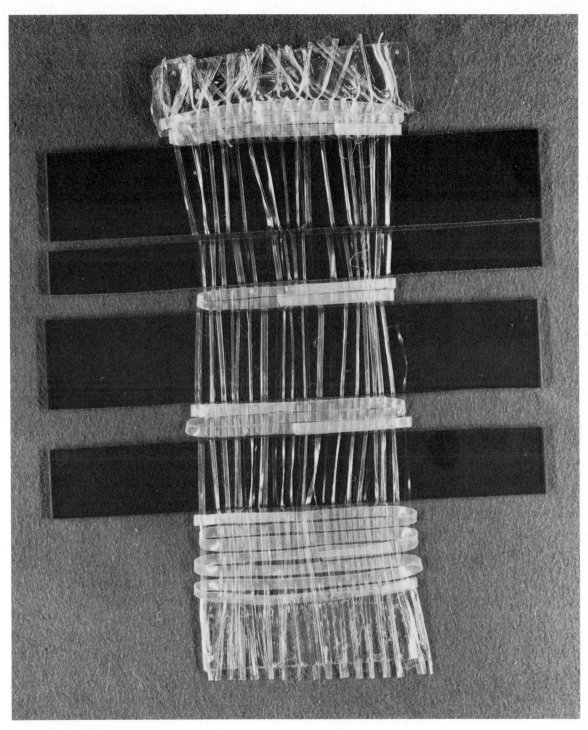

Fig. 118 Transparent warp with perspex and polythene weft

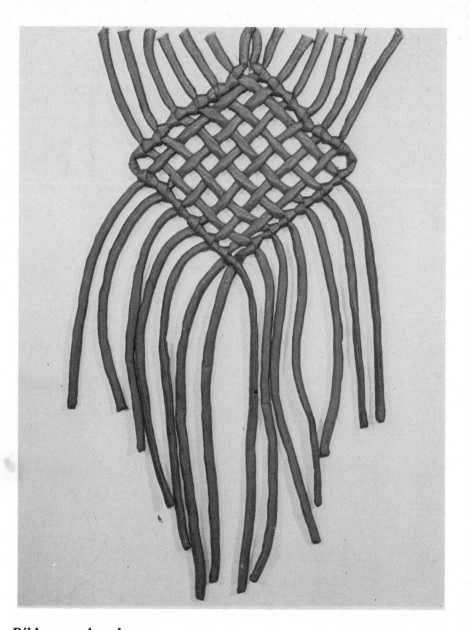

Fig. 119 Fabric rouleaux used as warp and weft

Ribbons and rouleaux

If velvet ribbon is alternated with strips of black sequins in both warp and weft the effect is very rich and these materials could be used for the collar and cuffs on an evening jacket, or, alternatively, to produce a simple garment, constructed in a similar way to the jerkin made with leather strips.

Fabric rouleaux can also be used to produce a decorative surface and these can either be left loosely interwoven as in fig. 119 or actually machined together. To machine the rouleaux in position, use a fine paper background that can be removed when the machining is finished.

Fig. 120   Chain linked
together

Fig. 121   Metal swarf
woven with cotton warp
and weft

Polythene

An interesting effect can be produced if strips of polythene are cut and then slits are cut in to them to coincide exactly with the position of the warp threads. The strip is woven in the usual way, then the flaps between the cut slits are encouraged to overlap the previous row. A fine Melinex can be used in the same way.

Working with metal

You could be forgiven for not believing that you can weave with metal, but it is possible and can produce very attractive results. I have woven metal parts from an old transformer with copper wire and coloured acetate. Chains can also be linked together in a form of interweaving. In fig. 120 the type of chain used is that without welded links. The reason for this is that sometimes links need to be opened, especially when starting and finishing a piece of work. Metal can also be woven through a normal yarn warp, either using straight rods or, as shown in fig. 121, using metal swarf. The pieces in the example were retrieved from a lathe that had been cutting mild steel.

Ideas for weaving materials   89

Bead weaving

Bead-weaving is really a separate section and has been partially dealt with in the chapter on needleweaving. Fig. 122 shows a bead loom with a thread warp and bead-weaving taking place. Figs. 123–125 demonstrate various stages of bead-weaving. The warp is composed of buttonhole thread and is used double at each outer edge.

To begin, work with the weft threaded through a beading needle and weave several rows at the beginning of the warp, using thread only. Count the number of spaces between your warp threads, and thread up with the same number of beads. Pass your beads under the warp and, using your forefinger, push a bead up through each warp space. Pass the beading needle back through the centre of the beads so that this time the thread passes across the warp and through the bead centres.

Designing a pattern

Sometimes it is difficult to visualize patterns. If you work on graph or squared paper, and make each square equal to a bead, then a design is easier to plan and work.

Fig. 122   A bead loom

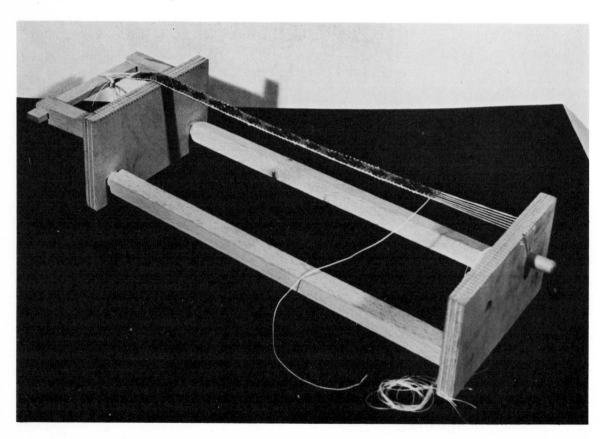

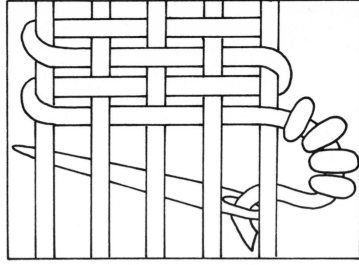

Fig. 123 Beginning to weave on a bead loom

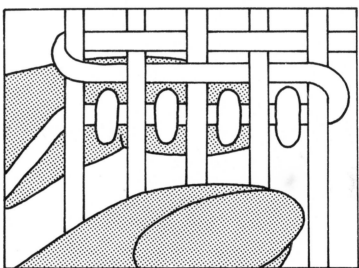

Fig. 124 Pressing the beads into place

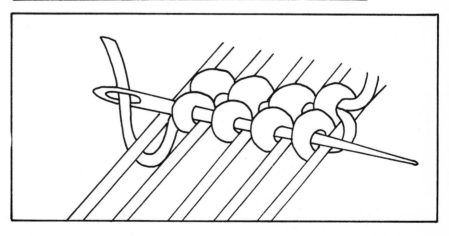

Fig. 125 Passing the beading needle through the beads

7 Texture

Textures in weaving are produced in two main ways. Either the yarn produces the texture or the fabric itself can be made to form textures. In some commercially produced ginghams and striped cotton fabrics there are areas where the fabric has been bubbled or rippled deliberately to enhance the design. Some of these ideas you can yourself reproduce either by cramming extra warp into an area or by weaving with a heavy yarn in the weft.

The other method of producing textures is by using what is known as a fancy yarn. This is a yarn that is looped, slubbed, hairy or decorative in some way. Using a fancy yarn is simple enough, fig. 58 shows a white mohair used with a slubby wool yarn.

Textures produced by looping

Looping the yarn itself is another method of producing textures. Some of these methods have already been explored: weft chaining in fig. 96 and soumak in fig. 95.

Various loops of weft can be pulled up in a straightforward plain weave and with a little forethought these loops can be used to create raised patterned areas. These loops, if arranged to lie vertically beneath one another, can then be chained together rather like weft chaining but in the opposite direction (fig. 126). To prevent the chained loops from unravelling, the final loop is held by a weft thread inserted through the loop.

The corduroy weave

In a similar way a corduroy weave can be used to create a pile fabric if you have a four-harness loom. Thread up your loom in a repeating pattern (see

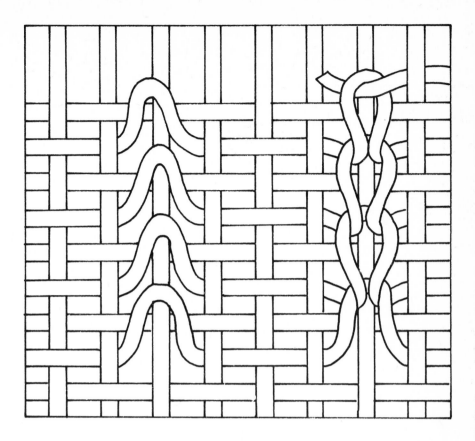

Fig. 126   Warp chaining

fig. 127). You will need a background weft which holds the fabric together and a pile-forming weft composed of six or more threads used as one and wound on one shuttle. The lifting pattern to produce corduroy is as follows:

First pick. Lift harnesses 1 and 3; use background weft.
Second pick. Lift harnesses 1; use pile weft.
Third pick. Lift harness 3; use pile weft.
Fourth pick. Lift harnesses 2 and 4; use background weft.
Fifth pick. Lift harness 2; use pile weft.
Sixth pick. Lift harness 4; use pile weft.

You can now see how the pattern is formed. Keep repeating these six picks. Sometimes odd ends of pile weft are left poking out of the main weaving. These ends will fit into the weaving because all the floating loops of pile weft are cut through at their centre points to form a Rya rug-type pile and any odd ends can be trimmed to match the pile. In the colour plate opposite page 56 a pile rug is shown woven in this way; the corduroy technique is interspersed with areas of plain weaving. Note that the pile in this rug has been cut at two different levels to give a stepped effect.

									4		4		4		4		4								
								3		3		3		3		3									
2		2		2		2		2												2		2		2	2
	1		1		1		1												1		1		1		1

Fig. 127   The thread-up a four-harness corduroy weave

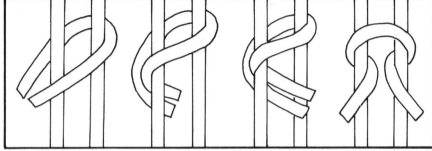

Fig. 128   A cut Ghiordes knot

Fig. 129   An unfinished rug on a rug frame

The Ghiordes knot

Another method of producing a pile effect is with the Ghiordes knot, either cut or uncut. Fig. 128 shows how to work a cut Ghiordes knot. In fig. 129 the uncut Ghiordes knot has been worked with a two-ply carpet yarn. The Ghiordes knot can also be uncut and a gauge of some kind used to keep the loop sizes even. Fig. 130 shows how to work an uncut Ghiordes knot with the gauge in position. This gauge can be anything from a knitting needle to a ruler or something larger, depending on the size of the loop required.

Wrapping the warp

Warp-wrapping, as the name suggests, is a method of wrapping yarn around the warp threads. This technique can be worked around one or several threads, in one colour to give textured effects, or in a variety of colours to give a striped effect. Depending on the position of the area to be wrapped one of two methods is used.

Method 1. The woven fabric is worked first and spaces are left in those places where weft-wrapping is to be worked. The yarn is wound around the individual warp threads travelling up one thread and down the next. The warp-wrapping thread is threaded through a large-eyed needle. The winding yarn is secured at each end of the wrapping process by passing it through the woven fabric at the top and bottom of each warp thread (see fig. 131).

Method 2. Refer to fig. 132 which shows a needle included in the wrapping area. When the wrapping is complete, the end of the thread is passed through the eye of the needle and the needle pulled through the wrapping. It is pulled through the side of the wrapping and any excess thread is trimmed off. Instead of using a needle, which can be rather thick, you could use a looped end of fuse wire.

Making a weft float texture

Textural patterning can be achieved by using weft floats. For example, if you look back to the corduroy weave at the beginning of this chapter and try to imagine that instead of cutting the loops that are formed you leave them to form a flat patterned texture, you will see the effects that can be obtained.

Another method is to work floats of weft on both sides of the fabric using a thicker yarn. This means that the float yarn is looped through the fabric on both the front and the back. A background cloth must always be woven, just as in the corduroy weave. This can be worked on a two-harness loom as the thicker floating yarn is put in, in a 'free-hand' way; in other words no harnesses are lifted and the weft is inserted by a shuttle over and under blocks of threads.

Fig. 130   Uncut Ghiordes knot

Fig. 131   Close-up of abstract tapestry showing wrapped warp (see colour plate opposite page 56).

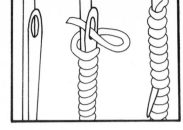

Fig. 132   Diagram showing the wrapped warp technique

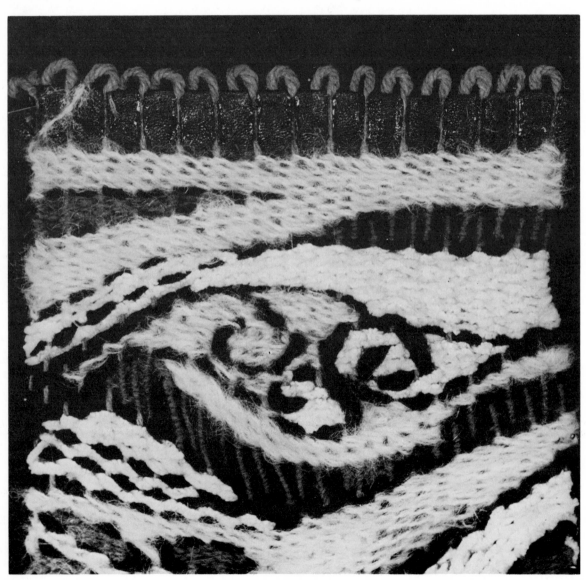

Weaving a double fabric

A double fabric can be worked on a four-harness loom using a straight thread-up. Basically, there are two fabrics which are woven at the same time in plain weave. One fabric is woven on the warp threads carried by harnesses 1 and 3 and the other fabric from threads carried by harnesses 2 and 4. Both fabrics are woven at the same time. If you are weaving your top fabric with a red weft and the underneath fabric with a black weft the following lifting pattern can be followed:

> *First pick*. Lift harness 1; use red weft.
> *Second pick*. Lift harness 3; use red weft.
> *Third pick*. Lift harnesses 1, 2 and 3; use black weft.
> *Fourth pick*. Lift harnesses 1, 3 and 4; use black weft.

By using the above lifting pattern, you should begin to see the separation of the warp into two fabrics. Obviously at some point the fabrics must be linked together to prevent them falling apart. This is done by reversing the lifting order to bring the warp threads of the underneath fabric to the top and vice versa.

> *First pick*. Lift harness 2; use black weft.
> *Second pick*. Lift harness 4; use black weft.
> *Third pick*. Lift harnesses 1, 2 and 4; use red weft.
> *Fourth pick*. Lift harnesses 2, 3 and 4; use red weft.

By reversing your lifting order every so often, you will obtain a ridged fabric, striped in red and black and completely reversible. Once you have mastered the technique of weaving a double fabric, you can experiment with different colours in the warp, arranged to complement your weft colours. Remember, one colour can be on harnesses 1 and 3, while a different colour is put on harnesses 2 and 4. The double fabric is then yet another way of giving a surface texture to a cloth.

The padded double fabric

By padding your double fabric in different sections you can create areas with different heights of ridges. To insert the padding you need to work an area of double cloth. When you have reached the point where the fabrics interchange, first open out the two fabrics by lifting the two harnesses involved in your first two picks—that is 1 and 3, or 2 and 4, depending on which fabric is on top. Pass through the two fabrics a piece of thick piping cord, sponge rubber, quilting material or anything that will act as padding. Close the two fabrics together and interchange them as already described. To weave a reasonable quality fabric you will find it necessary to put twice as many warp threads through each dent in the reed as you would normally do. If your fabric is rather thready, it is because the warp is too spaced out in the reed.

8 Three-dimensional weaving

In any form of three-dimensional work you will usually find it necessary to work on some sort of base. This base can be a removable frame, a framework that becomes part of the object, a padded base over which the basic object is worked, or some sort of supporting rod or shape that can be removed or not as desired.

The most straightforward three-dimensional weaving is that which is not really three-dimensional itself but merely decoration added to a three-dimensional object—chair seats, and deck-chair frames, for example, which can be worked in ways similar to the ideas shown in chapter 4.

To begin, work with the simplest three-dimensional shape and try a lampshade. An example of paper weaving on a lampshade is shown in fig. 14. Try using yarn instead of paper: you will find that paper tears easily while yarn will stand up to quite a lot of heavy handling (fig. 146).

A bottle is an easily obtained three-dimensional object, but bottles are not the easiest of items to weave on because of their slippery surfaces. However, try simple finger-weaving as shown in fig. 133. Always work in small sections which can be oversewn together when the work is completed. Adhesive tape can be used to anchor areas of weaving to the bottle surface while working. Fig. 134 shows the effect of finger-weaving in a belt.

Working a hat crown

A hat crown can be worked on a wig head or a millinery block. If a wig head is used it may need padding out a little with foam strips as usually the head sizes are rather small. You could try the finger-weaving method shown in fig. 133 or alternatively look again at some of the ideas in chapter 6. A crown could be woven in leather strips, and fig. 135 shows one way of beginning the

Fig. 133   Finger-weaving on a bottle neck

Fig. 134   A finger-woven belt

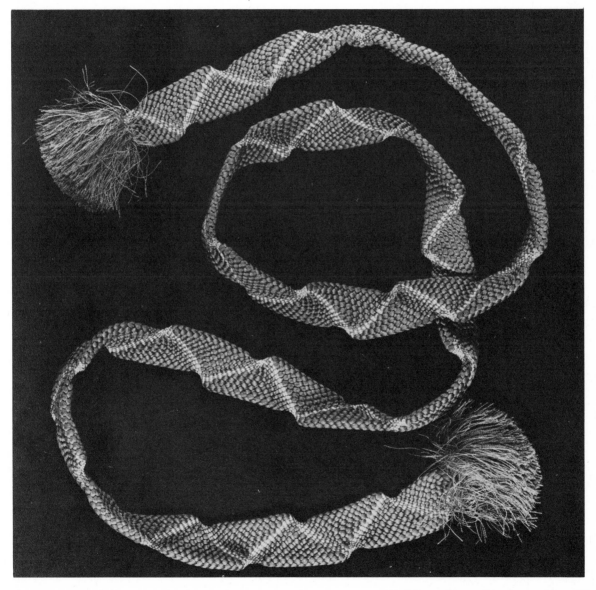

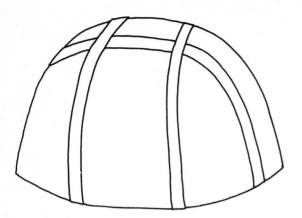

Fig. 135 *Starting a hat crown in leather strips*

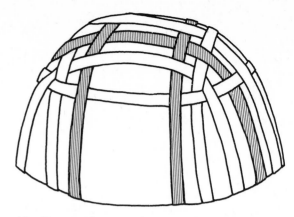

Fig. 136 *Further stages in working the hat crown*

crown using four strips, overlapped to form a double cross. Further strips are added a shown in fig. 59 until enough are in position to cover the side of the crown. Using these strips as if they were a warp, cut a series of lengths to use as a weft to encircle the side of the crown. The finished hat could have a solid leather brim or a woven one.

Ready-made three-dimensional shapes

Why not try working a portrait head over a wig block? The wig block could form the basic head shape and from this you could work features, hair and any other decoration over the block (fig. 137). Using a wig head has the particular advantage that pins can be stuck into the polystyrene foam, which makes the anchoring of threads much easier.

Look around for ready-made, three-dimensional objects, you will find them in the most unlikely places. The old bicycle wheel in fig. 138 was found on a rubbish dump. After being cleaned and painted with a matt black paint it was used as the basis for a piece of three-dimensional weaving. Some of the spokes were used for warp and various yarns used for the weft. The idea source was a stained glass window seen in Exeter Cathedral. Other ideas may occur to you, but if not, refer to the chapters on card and frame weaving for inspiration.

There are several traditional methods of producing three-dimensional weaving. The most well known is the 'corn dolly', which is woven from straw. This woven decoration, often seen in churches during harvest festival, would appear to have pre-Christian origins. The word 'dolly' is believed to be a corruption of the word 'idol'. Straw is a useful weaving medium because it is stiff and requires very little support. Fig. 139 shows some Chinese straw or grass-woven ornaments. The bird contains a wire support in the legs and neck but otherwise straw has been used throughout.

*Fig. 137   A head woven
over a wig block*

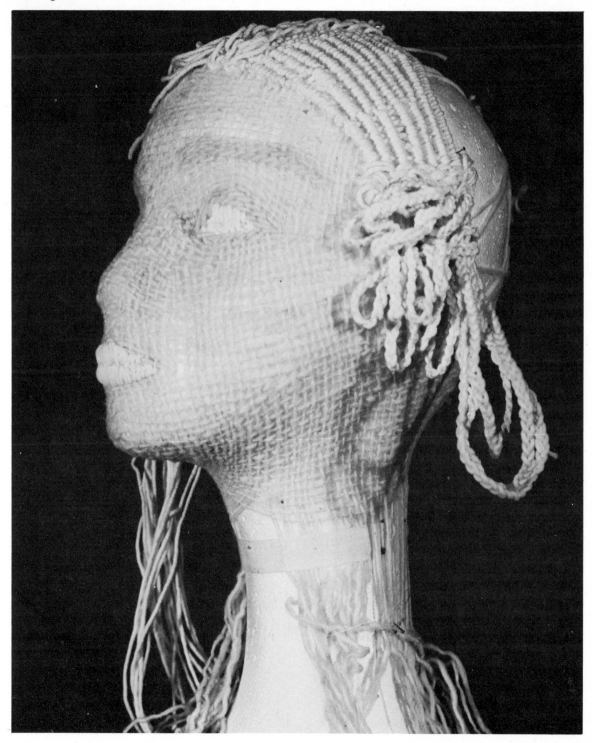

Fig. 138 Working on an
old bicycle wheel (see colour
plate opposite page 57).

Fig. 139 Chinese straw-
woven ornaments

Fig. 140   Working a
bangle

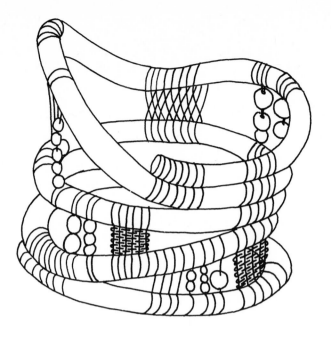

Making a bangle

To make a simple loom which at the same time becomes part of the finished object, you will need a length of fine metal tubing or wicker, as used in basketry. Make a circular shape large enough to slide over your hand to form a bangle, link several circular shapes together (as shown in fig. 140) and bind them together to hold the shape. Begin by interweaving between the circles, then use the threads formed as a warp and add weft where required. Beads can also be interwoven or left to form a decorative texture on the warp threads.

Making a three-dimensional loom

To make a large three-dimensional loom you will need the following equipment:

A central pole such as a broom handle.

Two circular half-inch plywood discs, with holes bored through the centre to fit the broom handle

Two metal holders—the type of attachments that are found in wardrobes for holding the clothes-hanging pole in position at each end.

A method of holding the broom handle in a vertical, rigid position. My base and pole originally held a wire dressmaking form so anything like this can be used.

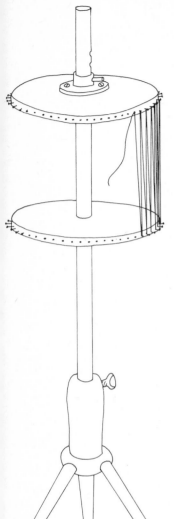

Preparing for weaving

Space nails around the edge of the plywood discs. Do not use heavy nails for this job or the wood will split. Then wind the warp between the nails as shown in fig. 141. To keep the plywood discs apart, first screw the hollow metal flanges, through which the broom handle passes, to the plywood discs and then drill them through the side. Drill a corresponding hole in the broom handle. These drilled holes can be placed in line to allow for the insertion of a dowelling peg. This peg prevents the disc from travelling up or down the broom handle. Arrange the flanges to face outwards at the top and bottom of the loom so that the dowelling pegs can be reached easily when the weaving needs to be removed from the loom.

Different diameters of disc could be used to produce varying shapes. Fig. 142 shows silhouettes of shapes which would be formed by using different disc sizes. The finished article could form a lampshade or an abstract, three-dimensional hanging.

There are many other methods of working in a completely abstract way. You can work without the use of frames or looms by allowing your material to dictate the finished shape. Materials like heavy rope which can be knotted or woven can be used, as can stiff materials like raffia and string, which lend themselves to working in abstract ways. These three-dimensional pieces begin to venture into the realms of free-form textile sculptures.

Fig. 141   Constructing a three-dimensional loom

Fig. 142   Possible shapes that can be woven on a three-dimensional loom

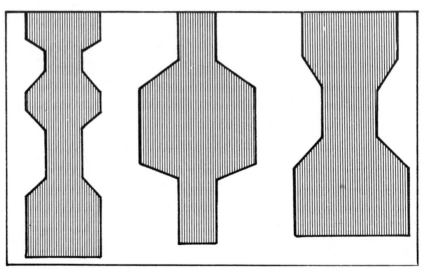

9 Weaving combined with other media

As the title suggests, this chapter is devoted to introducing some other textile techniques and how they can be combined with weaving. This chapter only really touches the surface of the possibilities that are available in combining textile techniques, but it is hoped that it will create an interest that will make you explore other textile methods in greater detail.

Macramé

Macramé is a form of knotting worked with hanging threads rather than a fixed warp. The threads are anchored at their top edge to a length of cord which is in turn pinned to a board. For practice purposes a piece of polystyrene can be used.

Horizontal cording

Fig. 143 shows horizontal cording. A separate cord is placed across the hanging threads and these threads are knotted around the cord as shown. Always make sure that the horizontal cord is held rigid.

Fig. 143 Horizontal cording in macramé

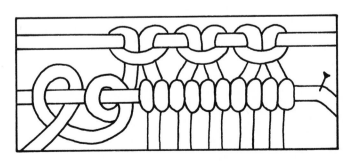

Diagonal cording

Fig. 144 shows diagonal cording. It is worked in a similar way to horizontal cording except the separate cord is pinned diagonally instead of horizontally. Sometimes, instead of using a separate cord, one of the hanging cords can be used.

The flat knot

Fig. 145 shows the stages of working the flat knot. Several of these knots can be repeated to form braid-like sinnets or, alternatively, single knots can be worked across the hanging threads in a row. To make an alternating pattern, work another row of knots below the first but use outside threads from adjacent knots to form the centre hanging threads, and the centre threads to make the actual knot. Fig. 146 shows a lampshade design worked in diagonal cording, weaving and flat knots.

These instructions for working macramé are, of necessity, rather brief, but you may find that your interest has been aroused enough to make you want to delve deeper into the craft. There are books that deal entirely with macramé techniques.

Fig. 144   Diagonal cording in macramé

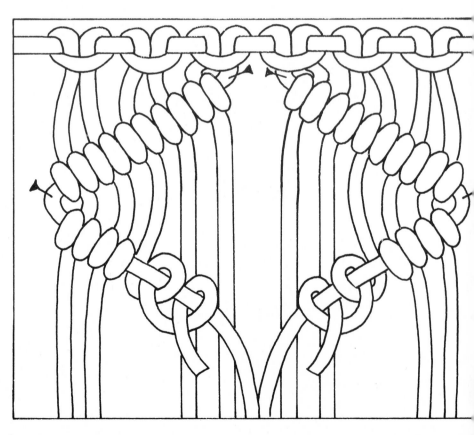

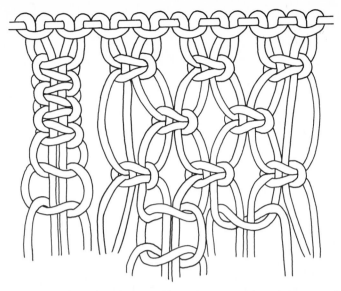

Fig. 145 The flat knot

Fig. 146 A white and gold lampshade

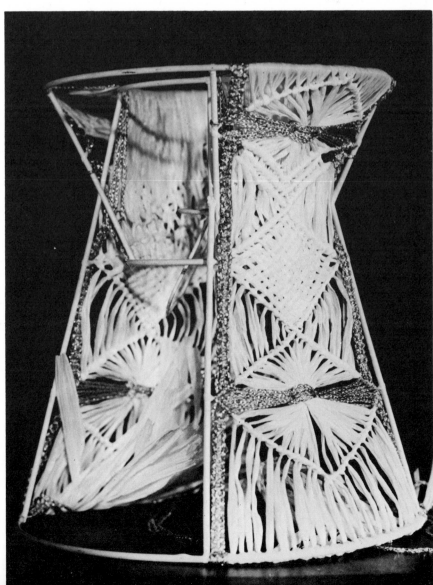

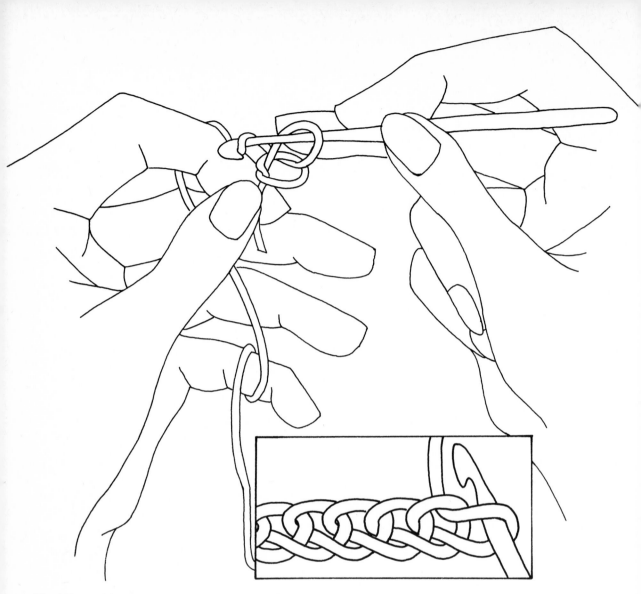

*Fig. 147 Making a chain
in crochet*

Crochet

Crochet is a method of making lace-like fabrics uing a simple hook and thread.

Making a chain

Fig. 147 shows how to begin in crochet by making a simple chain. The basic technique is to pass the crochet hook through the previous loop, pass your thread around the crochet hook and pull the thread through the loop. The loop formed is now used to pass the crochet hook through and so on. Once the chain is mastered there are a variety of simple stitches that can be worked. Among these are the slip-stitch, the double-crochet and the half-treble.

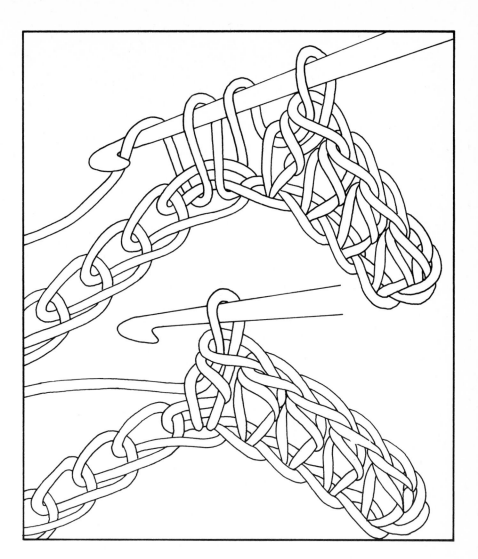

Fig. 148 The half-treble stitch in crochet

Half-treble

Fig. 148 shows how to make a half-treble. Make a basic chain and then, with a loop on your hook, put the thread over your hook, insert your hook into the chain, put your thread over the hook again, and draw through a looped stitch. You should now have three loops on your hook. Put the thread over the hook again and draw the thread through all the three loops, leaving one loop on the hook. You proceed along the chain working this series of movements into each chain loop.

Working a crochet chain into the warp threads

Fig. 149 shows the technique of working a crochet chain into the warp threads. The chain can be looped from warp thread to warp thread by inser-

Fig. 149 Working crochet loops into warp threads

Fig. 150 Combining crochet with weaving

110 *Imaginative Weaving*

ting several chains in between each thread or by passing from one thread to another, rather like weft chaining. Fig. 150 shows some examples of crochet worked into weaving.

There are many crochet patterns and only a few have been mentioned. There are many books that deal with the various techniques of crochet and for further details refer to these.

Plaiting

Plaiting is really a method of finger-weaving. Your threads are anchored at their top ends but left free at the bottom. Each thread, starting with the outermost, is interwoven through the adjacent threads. When all have been woven, the same procedure is used working from the opposite side; so there is a zig-zagging of threads through the braid that is formed. Individual plaits can be worked, as shown in fig. 151, or they can be linked together in two different ways. One method is to work a series of plaits side by side. Make them in multiples of even numbers—for example sets of four, six, eight, ten and so on. When you reach a point where you want linkage to take place, divide each plait in half and place adjacent halves from two plaits alongside one another, then plait these two halves together. A rather attractive net-like linkage occurs.

The second method of linking plaits is with areas of plain weave. Once again, work individual plaits and, when the required length has been worked, anchor the lower ends of the threads and work an area of plain weave. Plaiting can be commenced when desired. In fig. 152 the two methods are shown worked on a lampshade.

Fig. 151   Finger-weaving or plaiting

Fig. 152   Plaiting with weaving on a lampshade

Fig. 153   Working knitting with card-loom weaving

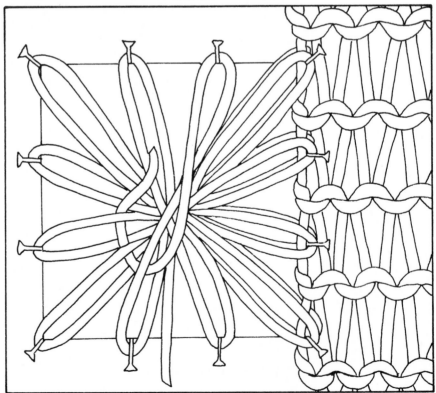

Knitting

Knitting will probably be familiar to most readers. Basically, it is a method of producing an interlaced fabric by using several needles and yarn.

Fig. 153 shows a square card loom with pins inserted along each edge. Work a flower motif as shown, around the pins beginning from the centre. Pass the loops at the edge of your knitting on to the pins on one side of the card. Do likewise on the opposite side. In the diagram, only one side is shown for clarity. Work another motif on top of the previous flower so that the knitted edge is now sandwiched between the two flower motifs. Using the length of thread that forms the motif, interweave around the centre area, where the threads of the flower motif cross one another. Weave enough to enclose the threads and stop them moving. To finish the edge, work a thread that knots the two halves of the flower motif together at a point where each pin is inserted. This secures the knitting permanently to the card weaving. The pins are removed when you have knotted all the four sides of the motif. These motifs can be inserted at intervals between the knitting or can themselves be joined together to form a strip of flower motifs. To do this, work the first flower motif as before, place both pieces of knitting in position then overlap the previous flower motif along one adjacent edge. When working the outer knotting thread, link in knitting, motif and knitting along three edges. Continue linking motifs and knitting in this way.

Sprang

Sprang is a method of producing an interlaced fabric by using threads stretched between two anchor points. This means that the technique is related more closely to weaving than any of the other methods described here. Superficially the technique appears to work like leno weaving, but it isn't really similar. Work this technique on a simple frame loom. Begin with several rows of plain weaving at each end of your loom. The sprang technique is to wind one thread with a neighbouring thread (see fig. 154). To prevent the threads from unwinding, insert a knitting needle as shown. All the threads across the warp are treated in this way. Leave the first knitting needle in position. Using a second knitting needle, intertwine another set of threads together across the warp. When the second needle is held in position remove the first. You should begin to see an intertwining pattern developing at each end of the loom. Once a definite pattern is formed, insert a few rows of plain weaving to hold the intertwining in position at each end of the loom. Continue the intertwining. Thus, in this way, identical patterns are created at each end of the loom. When no more intertwining can take place, insert a final piece of plain weaving at the centre point of your warp threads to keep all the intertwining in position. The work can be left on the frame, or alternatively removed, folded in half and sewn at each side to make an attractive bag (see fig. 155).

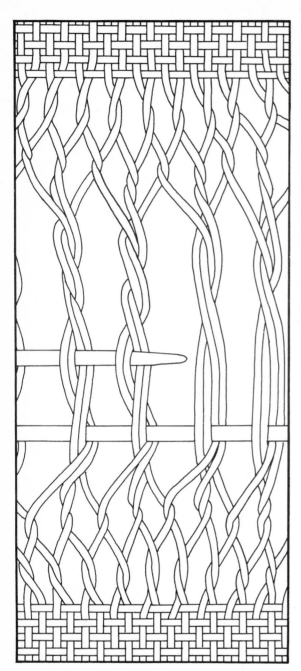

Fig. 154 Combining
sprang with weaving

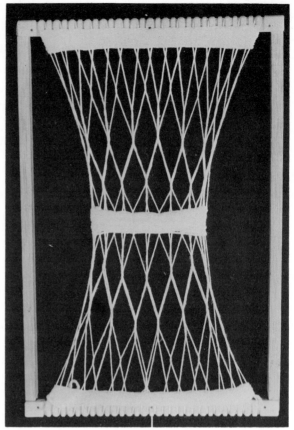

Fig. 155 Sprang com-
bined with weaving in a
frame

10 Inspiration

The sources from which ideas are derived are many and varied. They have been listed here under various headings: natural forms, man-made forms and accidental effects. There are probably many other headings that could be added in this section, but space does not permit their inclusion. It is hoped that the few ideas suggested in this chapter will spark off many ideas of your own.

Natural forms

This title covers everything from the smallest sea-shell to a whole landscape. There are different points to look for, depending on whether you are looking for an idea for a tapestry, a garment, a rug, or ideas for colour schemes and textures.

An original drawing of the structure of bone marrow was coloured in one of my experiments and from this a section was chosen and enlarged. The medium used for this enlargement was tissue paper, pleated and pinched to follow the flow of the bone structure, and some sunflower seeds. From this the more important shapes were traced off and the final drawing was used to produce a sample tapestry. The final result did not bear any obvious relationship to bone-marrow structure but it retained the important growth flow.

Try drawing some fruits and cutting through them to study the cross-section. By observing an orange cut in half, I was able to develop the collage of fabric and paper shown in fig. 156. This time the source of the idea is more obvious to see. This collage could equally well be used to produce a design for a circular rug.

The landscape too can provide inspiration. From a fairly straightforward

Fig. 156 Experiments, in-
cluding the cross-section of
an orange in collage. See
colour plate opposite
page 41.

Fig. 157 A painting of a
river with a tree and a fence

drawing of a river, with a lone tree and a fence the design in fig. 157 was produced. As you can see, no attempt has been made to reproduce a replica of the original, but it has been transformed into a series of flat abstract shapes which would make an excellent starting point for a tapestry hanging.

Man-made forms

Man-made forms are another useful source for ideas, whether they are sculpture, architecture, machine parts or whatever. The drawings of Winchester Cathedral (see figs 158–160) were all worked in different media. Each drawing shows a different aspect of the building. From these drawings an abstract, framed wall hanging was produced.

Stained glass windows were the inspiration behind fig. 138. The object itself was originally an old bicycle wheel.

Magazines and colour supplements are full of photographs, many of which may provide ideas, especially if you find you cannot draw or paint from the original object.

Fig. 158 Drawing in charcoal of Winchester Cathedral

Fig. 159 Drawing in pastels and paint of Winchester Cathedral

Accidental effects

Accidental effects are obtained in a number of ways. Try dribbling ink on to paper and then blowing the wet ink with a straw. Attractive, explosive shapes will result. Likewise, try dabbing different coloured paints on to a sheet of paper and then folding the paper; you will obtain unusual symmetrical patterns.

I tried tearing black paper in a haphazard fashion. Some of the paper was shiny, some matt black and some velvety in texture, but the most interesting effect formed where small areas of white were exposed in the tearing. The resulting design would have made a beautiful rug or hanging.

So next time you are bereft of ideas, try a visit to a museum, and take a sketch-book to note down colour ideas, textures or forms. If you are hesitant about drawing, most museums have a good selection of postcards of everything from fossils to plants, from geological strata and maps to stuffed birds.

If you are out walking in the town or in the country, observe what is around you. You could see an interesting piece of architecture, a carving or a sky-line or, in the country, a gnarled tree trunk, autumn leaves, or the flight of birds in the sky. All around you are sources for ideas. It is just a matter of keeping your eyes open.

Fig. 160   Drawing of Winchester Cathedral in white chalk on black paper

Type of yarn	Purpose or end-product
All types of cotton	Place mats, bags, cushion covers.
Any yarn	Decorative wall panels
Lightweight wool	Garments
Lightweight cotton	Garments
Raffia	Place mats, wall hangings, bags.
Two-ply rug wool	Rugs, cushion covers.
Medium-weight wool	Garments, bags, accessories such as scarves.
Wool/nylon mixtures	If heavy weight—rugs; if light weight—garments.
Man-made fibres	Lightweight (e.g. nylon knitting wool) for garments and wall hangings.
Polythene	Wall hangings, room dividers, window hangings and 'fun' garments.
String	Bags, rugs, wall hangings.
Leather	Bags, slippers, garments, cushion covers, wall hangings.

Index